The DIY Balloon Bible Themes & Dreams

...How to Decorate for Galas, Anniversaries, Banquets, & Other Themed Events!

By Sandi Masori, CBA

Copyright 2017 Sandi Masori,
All Rights Reserved

ISBN 13: 978-1981311040
ISBN 10: 1981311041

Forward

Dear reader, thank you so much for your continued support for my books and videos. These are truly a labor of love and I work really hard to put so much information into this format. The book is designed to give you the basics, a jumping off point if you will. Every "recipe" has a companion video so that you can either read it, or watch it. Many of you will add your own touches and embellishments to the designs and that's great!

I'd love to see your pictures. I run a Facebook group called DIY Balloon Art, where you can share your photos, ask for advice, enter fun contests and network with other balloon pros, and diyers who share your passion. Here's the link...

http://www.Facebook.com/Groups/DiyBalloonArt

I also want to offer you the opportunity to see some of the videos for the chapters that had to get cut out of the book because of the size. I figured that 400 pages might just be a little overwhelming ;-). If you would like to see those videos, and download some extra recipes, a glossary and other goodies, visit

http://BalloonUtopia.com/ThemesDreams/

and fill out the form. This goes to an automated system and will trigger the system to send you a private link to the membership page where those extra goodies live. The resulting email does come from an automated system so if you don't get it within 10 minutes or so, check your junk mail for an email from me.

At the time of this books publication, I'm already hard at work on the next volume. I love to hear from you guys, so let me know what other types of designs you want to see.

And of course, subscribe to my You Tube channel so that you can see all the new tutorial videos I put out every week. ;-)

Xoxox <3
Sandi

Table Of Contents

Forward iii
Table Of Contents iv
Acknowledgements vii

The Basics 1
How to Make a Balloon Column Frame 2
Balloon Arch Frame 4
Building Blocks of Balloons 6
How to Make a Balloon Sizer Box 11
How To Tie Duplets 14

60's / 70's Theme 17
Flower Power Balloon Tower 18
Woven Flower 22
Linky Flower Column 26
Psychedelic Flower 30
Psychedlic Tunnel 35
Hollywood Theme 39

Hollywood Star Stantions 40
Star Tower 44
Star Arch 48
Golden Awards Statue 51
Hollywood Theme Photo Op Station 58

www.DiyBalloonArt.com

Candyland Theme 63
Balloon Candy 64
Balloon Lollipop 66
Candy Tower 70
Giant Candy Cane 73
Giant Milkshake Balloon Sculpture 81

Out-of-This World Theme 87
Astronaut 88
Twisted Rocket Ship 94
Ray Gun 99
Planets 103
Twisted Star 106
Alien Airplane 110

Out-of-This World Photo Frame 116
Monster Theme 121
Monster Totem Pole 125
Casino Theme 133
Casino Tower 134
Poker Centerpiece 137
Casino Theme Balloon Arch 142
Poker Chip Selfie Frame 145

Mardi Gras Theme 149
Giant Mardi Gras Mask 150
Mardi Gras Centerpiece 153
Mardi Gras Beaded Arch 157
Awareness Themes 163

Mini Awareness Ribbon 164
Giant Awareness Ribbon 166

Elegant Themes / Events 173
Elegant Lighted Centerpiece 174
High Heel Shoe 178
Glitter Balloon 183
Champagne Demi Arch 185
Jumbo Color - Changing Balloon Lights 190
Organic Photo Frame – Full Size 194

Appendix & Resources 198
Guest Contributors 199
About The Author 200

Acknowledgements

It's hard to believe that this is my sixth book and the fourth in the DIY BALLOON BIBLE series. Just a few short years ago I would never have believed that I would write a book, let alone six! There are so many people who have guided, led and helped me along the way, so I want to give them a huge shout out and my undying gratitude.

First and formost, I want to thank my family. My kids, who have been through so much this past year, and managed to come through it without too much damage (I hope). They have modeled for the book, popped balloons, held cameras, cleaned up after me, and generally are pretty awesome!

My parents, who have been an amazing support for me this year, and my whole life really, if I'm being honest. I don't know what I would have done without their help driving, and teaching driving for that matter.

My brother from another mother (and father), John Finley, who is an amazing surrogate uncle and playmate for the kids, keeping them happy and busy so I could work.

My cousin Jessica, who has helped out with doing things with the kids and drop offs and pick ups so I could work.

My amazing assistant Mary, without whom I would be a mess. She manages to keep me organized and on track, not an easy feat.

My former assistant Carlos, who still allows me to call on him when I need help, in spite of having a full time job and an exciting new career path.

My videographer, GS Ford, who makes himself available everytime I get the urge to make more videos.

Rod Kim and Vince Cirino, from the romantic pop duo RKVC. They have come in and helped me out in more ways than I can count- by helping me with my shoots, lending me their music for my videos, editing my videos and more.

My dear friend Jeff Fu, from Wreckless Eating, who has helped me as DP on my shoots, given me great advice about my you tube channel, and gave me a great deal on some camera equipment.

Dustin Parker and Sara Warner who also have stepped in to help me complete the videos for this book.

My mentors, Clint Arthur and Mike Koenigs, without whom I never would have written a book or made any of my 70+ TV appearances.

My book clients, who keep me motivated to write more books because they are rocking it with theirs.

My balloon clients, who keep challenging me with new décor requests that eventually make it into my books.

The balloon community and my You Tube fans, without your support, there would be no reason for me to do what I do.

My friend Rachel Porter who co-authored the first DIY BALLOON BIBLE with me, and acts as a sounding board for me all the time. She also helps me teach the balloon business bootcamp course.

My guest artists; Caity Byrne of All About Balloons, John Justice of Splendid Balloons and Darren Saari of Twiisted Balloons. They gave up their time and knowledge to make this book better.

My readers, without you buying these books, there would be no reason for me to keep writing them.

There are so many other people who deserve recognition, probably too many to list, so to everyone who wasn't mentioned by name, you are no less important or appreciated. A huge "Thank you" to you all.

The Basics

How to Make a Balloon Column Frame

Materials:
- Piece of wood, square, cut to size needed, painted black
- Flange, painted black
- Threaded pipe
- EMT, coated black

Screw the flange down to your piece of wood. Once you have the flange attached, screw yo ur threaded pipe into the flange. The size is going to depend on what you're doing. I generally use ¾" and then I use ½" EMT.

Then get your EMT. I generally cut them to 7', some cut them to 5'. They come in 10' lengths. Take your pole and simply insert onto your screw. Then put a piece of duct tape where it connects. That's going to make a good, sturdy base plate and pole.

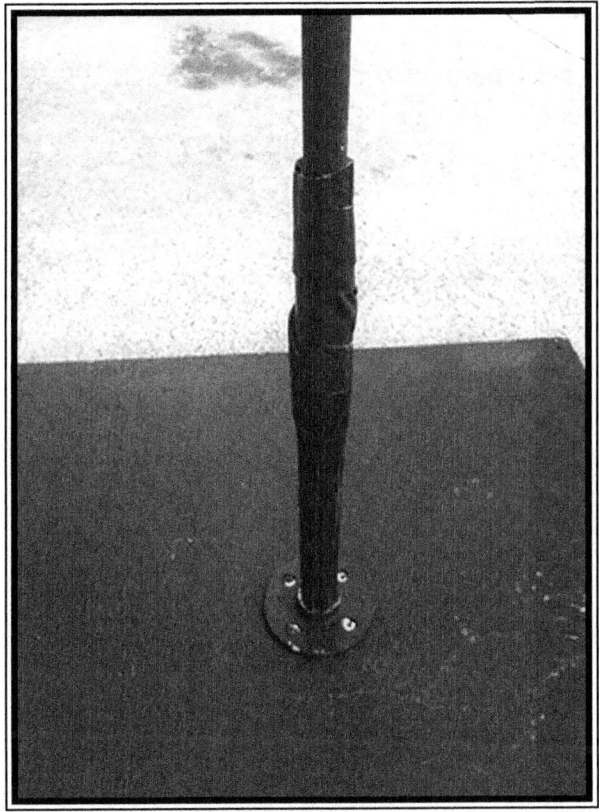

For columns or arches that may go outdoors, or in heavy traffic areas, use a larger piece of wood for a bigger footprint. I recommend 2' by 2'.

If you're trying to make a centerpiece, I would recommend cutting your wood to 10" x10" or 12" x 12".

Balloon Arch Frame

Materials:

- Two 2x2 square piece of wood
- Two Flanges
- Two Threaded pipes
- Two ½" EMT, 4'
- Three ¾" gray PVC, schedule 40, 8' lengths

Make sure to cover any raw metal edges with balloons or duck tape.

Place the flange into the middle of your square of wood, screw it down.

The threaded pipe goes into the flange.

Place your 4' piece of EMT into the threaded pipe. You can tape to secure. Make sure to tape on a diagonal. This is your base. Make two.

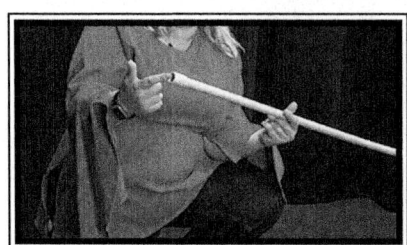

Gray PVC has bells on the end, so that you can connect them together without needing an extra piece. One of your three pieces will not have the bells on the end. This is the middle piece, and it will connect to the bells on either end piece.

Place a piece of tape at the center of your center piece of PVC. This will be the very center of your arch.

Connect your three pieces of PVC. You can tape the joints if you want.

Slide each end of the PVC over the EMT on the bases to create your arch.

If you do not have ¾" PVC, use duct tape and/or zip ties to attach the PVC to the EMT. If you use zip ties and cut the ends, make sure to cover the raw edges with tape to prevent sharp edges from popping balloons. If you leave the edges long you can tuck them into the balloons to hide them.

Don't be afraid to use too much tape. You can always use a knife to cut it down later.

Building Blocks of Balloons

We're going to talk about the building blocks of balloons, some of the different kinds of balloons and some of the different techniques.

We'll start with Linky balloons. These are so much fun. They've basically got a tail on both ends, so they have your nozzle side so you can blow into it, and then they've got a little tail on the end here so that you can attach things to it or do all kinds of crazy things.

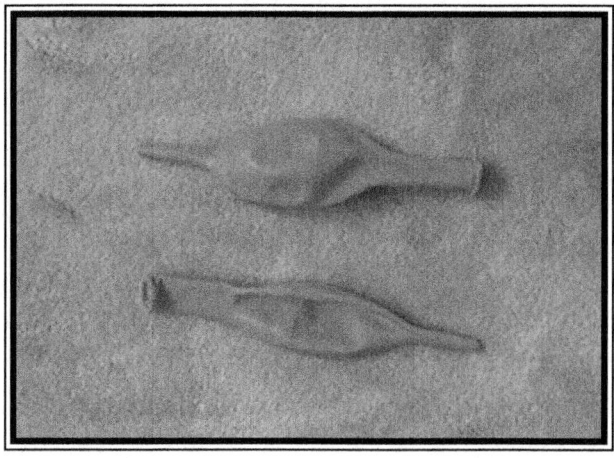

There's a lot of different ways to size your balloons. Another way to size your balloons is to count how many pumps you're doing with your balloon pump, because if you're doing 10 pumps and you do 10 pumps on every balloon then it's going to be the same size. Every Linky balloon that I do 10 pumps on should come out to be the same size.

If you've never used a balloon pump before, when you use the balloon pump you want to put the balloon all the way onto the pump, and then you can't just start pumping because it's going to fly away. What you need to do is actually hold it onto the pump while you pump it. It seems obvious enough, but this is actually one of the most common mistakes and frustrations that I see people making.

Also, make sure that the handle is all the way down, so that you get a full stroke in each direction.

Here's another mistake that I see people making, they'll try to pump it, especially with the 260s, and the balloon will be folded down on the pump, and they're wondering why it's not going. Where's the air going to go, if they've sealed off the chamber? You want to make sure that you're blowing straight into the bowl of the balloon, or in the case of one of the long skinny balloons straight into the tube.

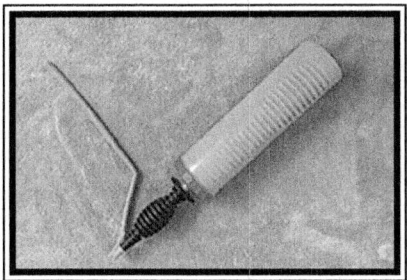 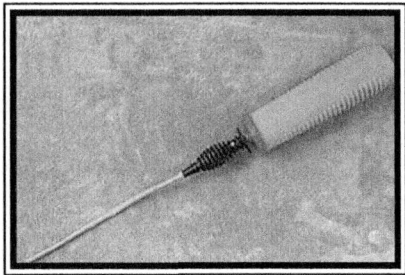

Remember to do a full pump from the bottom all the way to the top.

With Linky balloons we can tie them together in a lot of ways.

Tying two balloons together is called a duplet. The building block of balloon décor is duplets. If you take two duplets and put them together, then you have a quad. This is what we build a lot of our decorations on, quads. Quads are a really important part of balloon decorations.

If you were to take a single balloon and tie it into a quad then you would have a five pack. Five packs can be a huge pain in the butt to work with, but they can be really effective for holding things stably or when you need it to look a little bit rounder.

If you really want it to look round then you're going to want to do a six pack, which I will tell you that the first three six packs that you put onto a pole are a pain in the butt, because one of them always wants to pop up. You've just got to have patience, and you've got to just keep working it and keep playing with it until you get it.

Now let's talk about the non round balloons. There's a lot of different shapes and sizes. We have donuts. We have blossoms. We have hearts. All of those pretty much act the same as round balloons.

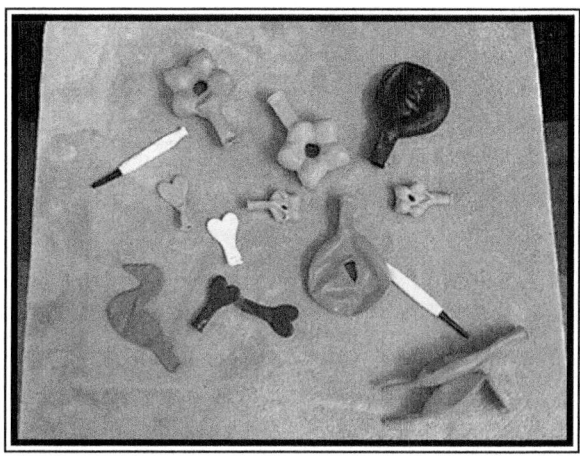

The long balloons act differently. A 160 when fully inflated is approximately 1" wide and 60" long. A 260 when fully inflated is approximately 2" wide and 60" long. A 350 is approximately 3" wide and 50" long. A 646 is approximately 6" wide and 46" long.

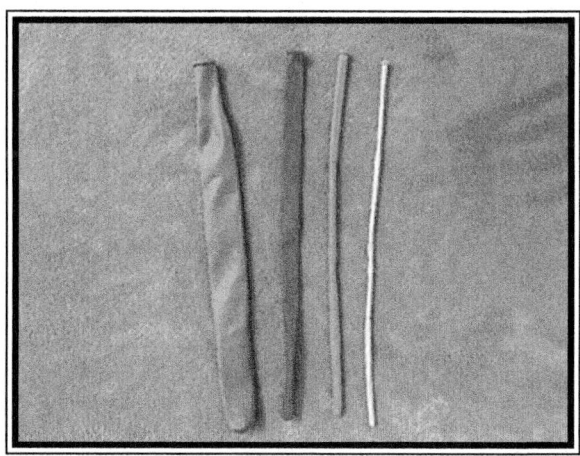

When you fully inflate a balloon and it is very taut you cannot put a twist in it. Usually when we blow up these kinds of balloons before we tie them we give it a burp. What that means is we just let some air out. If I want to use the balloon fully inflated this will work if you only need one twist. If I was going to make a flower, and I needed to have a lot of pressure and have six twists in it, this would be too tight. You want to play with the pressure.

When I'm teaching people in person, I give them a 260, and tell them to inflate it until it pops. That's what I want you to do at home too. The reason is that you need to get the feel for how much the balloon can take, and how much is too little pressure to keep it inflated to the end. Popping a few balloons by overinflating will teach you more about the right way to inflate than any book could.

It's really hard to get a lot of twists in a 646, because they're pretty thick. It's pretty rare that you can do more than one or two twists in one. These are most stable when you're using it as a single balloon or as a single piece. There's a lot of things that we do using this 646s or 660s for the base of a pedestal.

Everybody has a different way to tie it. For the non round balloons I lay it across my hand between my middle finger and my ring finger, and I bring it around the back of my index finger and my middle finger until it crosses. Then I kind of open up my fingers so I can push it through, and I pull it and pull my fingers out. That's how I tie. If you ask five balloon twisters you're going to get five different ways to tie.

The 646 has another really cool property to it. That is that because they're long and heavy. When it's fully inflated, if you put your four fingers and push the end inside, then if you let go these fly off. That's something really fun. Once one of those comes out at a party they're kind of zooming all over the place. Kids love this!

How to Make a Balloon Sizer Box

Materials:
- Box
- Ruler
- Pen
- Box cutter

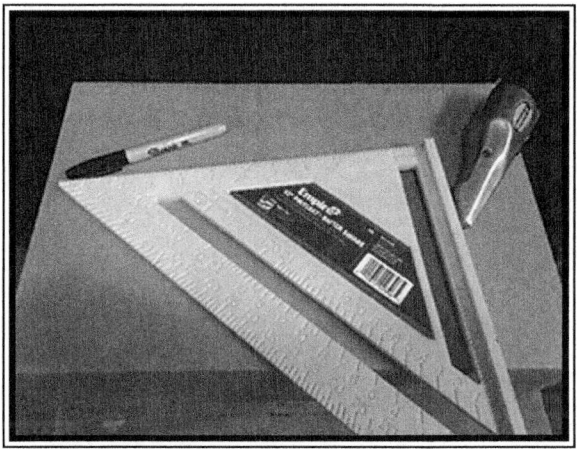

First, get a box. Then decide what size balloon you are trying to make. Cut a hole to the size that you want to make your balloon. Don't worry about trying to cut a round hole, It's a lot easier to cut a square hole. Just measure to the size you want and cut it out with a box cutter.

Then inflate your balloon and overinflate it. Slowly let air out until it just slips through the box. When it just passes through the hole, then you've got the right size.

If you're doing a lot of balloons you might want to have two boxes or have multiple people doing it.

If you have to force it in, it's too big, and if it goes in too easily it's too small. It should just go into the box.

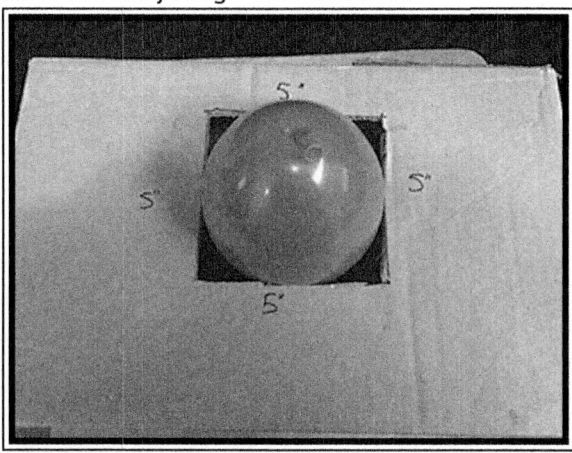

To See The Companion Video Go To:
https://youtu.be/Y6GBIA34KtA

How To Tie Duplets

Materials:
- Two balloons

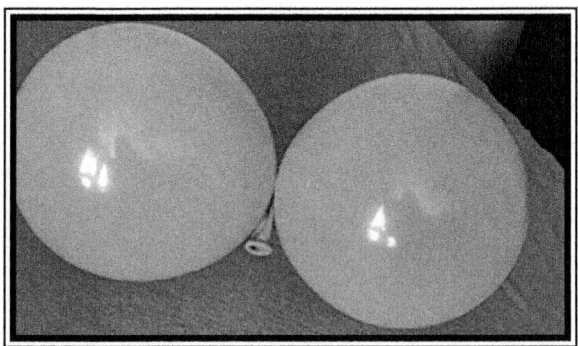

Take the nozzle ends of two balloons and hold them together. Wrap around each other twice, and then tie a knot. You always want to pull on the nozzle side to tighten, and never on the balloon, because that could put a friction tear.

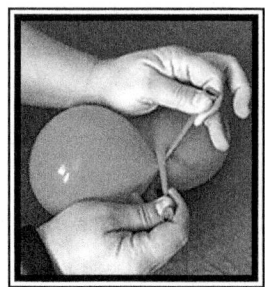 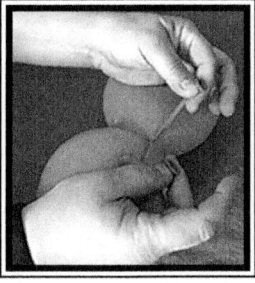 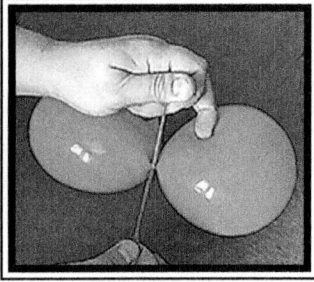

Everybody ties a different way, and as many balloon artists as you ask, that's how many different ways you're going to see to tie.

Wrapping around twice makes a tighter connection point, so there's less chance of air leaking.

The DIY Balloon Bible Themes & Dreams

To See The Companion Video Go To:
https://youtu.be/uoATLKlwDdg

60's / 70's Theme

Flower Power Balloon Tower

Materials:
- Base plate and 7' pole
- 56 11" balloons, inflated to 8.5"
- 20 wildberry
- 10 lilac
- 6 yellow
- 20 lime green

Recipe from bottom – all clusters are based on 4 balloons

1. 11" lime green balloons inflated to 8.5"
2. 11" wildberry balloons inflated to 8.5"
3. 2 – 11" wildberry balloons and 2 – 11" yellow balloons, inflated to 8.5"
4. 11" wildberry balloons inflated to 8.5"
5. 11" lime green balloons inflated to 8.5"
6. 11" lilac balloons inflated to 8.5"
7. 2- 11" lilac balloons inflated to 8.5", and 2- 11" yellow balloons inflated to 8.5"
8. 11" lilac balloons inflated to 8.5"
9. 11" lime green balloons inflated to 8.5"
10. 11" wildberry balloons inflated to 8.5"
11. 2- 11" wildberry, and 2- 11" yellow balloons inflated to 8.5"
12. 11" wildberry inflated to 8.5"
13. 11" lime green balloons inflated to 8.5"
14. 11" lime green balloons inflated to 8.5"

Start with a quad of green balloons. Wrap this on the base of the pole.

Now take a quad that is four pink balloons. Wrap this on top of the green quad.

The next quad has the center of the flower, so it is two pink balloons and two yellow balloons. Wrap this onto the pole. Make sure that the two yellow balloons are opposite each other.

Wrap another full pink quad onto the pole. You have created your first flower shape.

Wrap on another green quad, so that each flower is separated by the green.

Now take your solid lilac quad and wrap it in. Next use the quad that has lilac and yellow. Again, arrange so that the yellow balloons are opposite each other. Top with another solid lilac quad.

Wrap in another solid green quad.

Continue up the pole in this pattern, alternating flowers and green quads. End with a green quad at the top of the pole.

**To See The Companion Video Go To:
ttps://youtu.be/C-RlH0EMsS4**

Woven Flower

Materials:
- Three 260 balloons, fully inflated and burped
- One 260 balloon, inflated 3/4

Tie one of the fully inflated 260s into a circle.

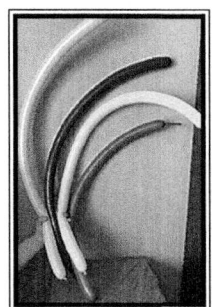 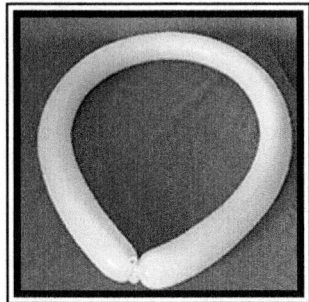 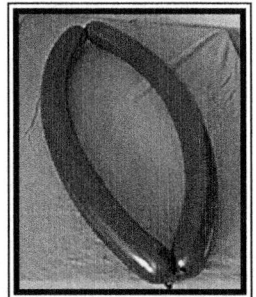

Find the center across from the knot. Pinch and twist one side.

Push the two ends together toward the middle and twist. You should have a figure eight shape. Wrap the nozzle around the center to secure. Set aside.

Do the same thing with the other two fully inflated 260s.

Take the three 260s and twist them together in the center. Arrange the loops in the pattern you want.

Hold two of the loops. Put your right hand through the right side loop and grab the left side loop. Put your left hand through the left side loop and grab the right loop. Gently pull your hands out through the loops, so that the loops become interlocked.

Working around, continue doing the same thing, interlocking each of the loops.

Gently arrange and press to get the shape that you want and flatten the flower.

Take the partially inflated 260. Twist off a bubble at the nozzle end. This is the stem.

Put the 260 into the center of the flower. Gently work the bubble into the center of the petals.

Make a small pinch twist in the stem on the back side of the flower. That changes the direction, so that the stem points straight down.

Fold the bottom of the stem up. Squeeze and twist. Feed the end through the loop you just made. Make a small pinch twist. This is a leaf. Squeeze to shape.

If you have any tail left in the stem, tie it off and remove the excess.

To See The Companion Video Go To:
ttps://youtu.be/BJJSv-mxoql

Linky Flower Column

Materials:
- Base plate and pole
- 11" balloons, tied in duplets
- 11" Linky balloons, tied in duplets
  260 balloons, fully inflated and burped

Create a quad with a duplet of 11" round balloons and a duplet of 11" Linky balloons. Arrange so that the balloons alternate.

Wrap the quad onto the base of the pole.

Wrap a second quad on top of the first.

Continue packing the column with quads just like the first, arranging so that the balloons spiral up the pole.

To create the flowers, take a 260 balloon and tie into a circle.

Straighten it out to find the center point. Pinch one side and twist.

While holding the 260 flat, split it approximately into thirds. Squeeze and twist.

Fold each twist so that you have a Z shape.

While holding your hands on the twists, squish them together and twist around. This creates a six petal flower. Do the same with other 260s.

Tie the flowers onto the Linky balloons in the column, wrapping the end of the Linky balloon around the center of the flower to secure it.

The DIY Balloon Bible Themes & Dreams

**To See The Companion Video Go To:
https://youtu.be/wO_MGgmUTbU**

Psychedelic Flower

Materials:
- Base plate and pole
- Eight 260s balloons, green
- Sixteen 4" round balloons, green, quads
- Ten Linky Sprays
- Five 4" balloons, red
- One smiley face balloon
- Uninflated 260

Wrap two 4" quads at the base of the pole.

Spiral wrap up the pole with 260s. Tie the 260s into duplets, and then a quad. Wrap the quad of 260s between the two layers of 4" quads. Pull each 260 up between each balloon in the 4" quad.

Twist two 260s together in a spiral. Wrap the spiral around the pole and secure to the pole.

Take the third 260 and spiral it up around the pole in the same way. Repeat with the final 260.

Wrap two quads of 4" balloons to the pole at the top of the 260 spiral.

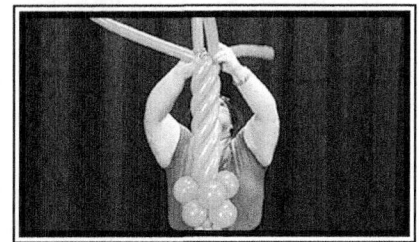

Repeat the spiral process with four more 260s, securing them to the top of the pole. Wrap the 260s around each other several times to secure. Deflate the excess 260s and tie off.

Create a quad with Linky balloons. Tie in a single balloon to create a quint. These are the five petals of your flower. Create a second quint just like this.

Make a quint out of the 4" red balloons.

It's best to use like number groups for your flower so that they nestle together.

Tie the smiley face balloon into the middle of your 4" quint.

Attach an uninflated 260 to the back of the smiley face.

Arrange your two quints of Linky balloons on top of each other. Place the 4" quint with the smiley face on top. Take the uninflated 260 and stretch it between the Linky balloons until it reaches the bottom. Figure eight it around the layers to secure.

Attach the flower to the step with one of the 260 ends at the top of the pole that you deflated and tied off. Wrap the uninflated end around the middle of the flower to secure.

Caity Byrne is the CEO of All About Balloons, a nationwide balloon décor service. If you want to learn more about Caity or All About Balloons, visit her website at

http://www.AllAboutBalloons.com

To See The Companion Video Go To:
https://youtu.be/xHwC8nfkyew

Psychedlic Tunnel

Materials:
- Linky balloons
- 5" balloons, tied in sets of three
- 5" balloons, tied in duplets
- Forty 10" balloons, tied in group of five
- Forty 8" balloons, tied in group of five
- Water weights

Tie Linky balloons into four strings of 13 balloons. Make sure that there is a nozzle at each end.

Make 11 chains of three Linky balloons.

Tie a set of three 5" balloons onto each end of a chain of three Linky balloons.

Wrap duplets around the two center joins. Do the same for all 11 chains.

Use the 5" balloons at the end of the three Linky chain to join the 13 balloon chain. Wrap around the first knot.

Add each string of 13 balloons to the three Linky chain, using the 5" balloons to wrap around and secure.

Arrange so that the chains lay with the 13 balloon chains parallel and the three balloon chain connecting them across the top.

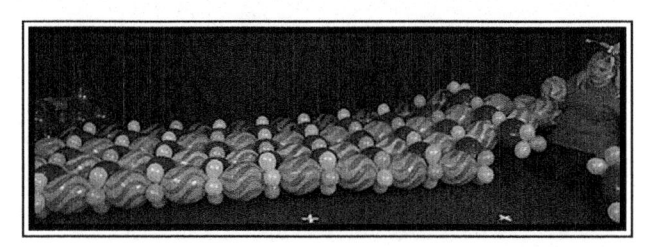

Continue wrapping a shorter three balloon chain across the longer chains at each knot. Remember to use the 5" balloons to wrap around, as they are easier to replace than the larger balloons if popped.

Take a set of five 10" balloons and a set of five 8" balloons and twist them together. Arrange so that the smaller balloons sit on top of the larger balloons. This creates a pocket at the bottom. Create eight bases like this.

Tie a water weight to the end of one of the long chains.

Stretch the water weight down and push it into the base of 8" and 10" balloons that you created. The water weight should nestle into the pocket at the bottom.

Do the same at both ends of each long chain.

To See The Companion Video Go To:
https://youtu.be/kSXGHyHO6GU

Hollywood Theme

Hollywood Star Stantions

Materials:
- 3 Lamp bases, 4' tall
- Eight 11" balloons sized to 9", tied in duplets, Color A
- Eight 11" balloons sized to 7", tied in duplets, Color B
- Twelve 5" balloons sized to 4", tied in duplets, Color A
- Twelve 5" balloons sized to 4", tied in duplets, Color B
- Foil Star balloon, 18" or 20"
- Uninflated 260s
- 6" Linky balloons

Use an uninflated round balloon on the top of your lamp base to prevent it from popping the balloons.

Take two duplets of 9" balloons in Color A and twist them together into a quad. Twist the quad onto the base of the pole.

Take two duplets of 7" balloons in Color B and twist them together into a quad. Wrap the quad onto the top directly above the first quad.

Take a 4" duplet of Color A and a 4" duplet of Color B and twist them together to create a quad. Wrap onto the pole so that the colors alternate. Continue wrapping five more 4" duplets up the pole, spiraling the colors as you go.

Wrap a 7" quad in Color B onto the pole above the last 4" quad.

Wrap a 9" quad in Color A onto the pole above the 7" quad.

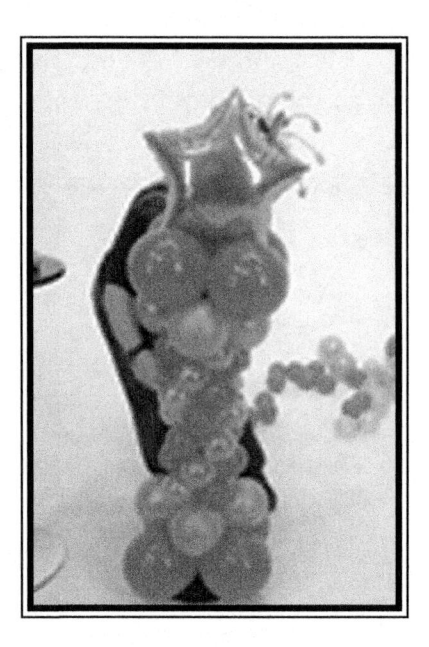

Tie an uninflated 260 just under the valve of the foil star balloon. Use the 260 to attach the star to the top of the column. Bring the 260 under the top two quads and figure eight it around to secure.

Tie Linky balloons together to create a chain. Tie one end of the chain to one of the nozzles of the top quad on your pole. Tie the other end to the top of a second column. Repeat with more columns and chains to create your row of stations.

**To See The Companion Video Go To:
https://youtu.be/PxFxWyeXhag**

Star Tower

Materials:
- Base plate and pole
- Twenty-seven 11" balloons, sized to 8.5"
- Nine 18" foil stars
- One 36" foil star

Tie together an 11" latex balloon and a foil star. This is not easy. You want to hold the foil part and use the latex to wrap around. Try to create a circle with the latex and the foil, and roll the knot through and pull tight. Make sure to tie the latex balloon under the valve of the foil balloon.

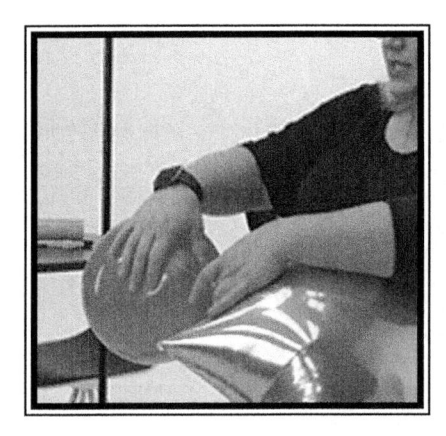

Make nine latex duplets.

Every layer of your tower will have one star and three latex balloons.

Wrap the star and latex duplet around the base of the pole. Lock it in by placing the latex duplet on the base and wrapping it around the pole to secure.

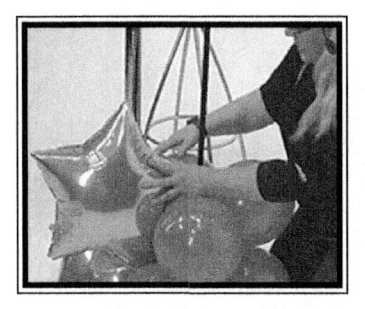

The star is not going to lay flat.

Continue up the pole just as you would with a regular column, using a star and latex duplet and a latex duplet. It will take some adjusting to get the balloons to lay the way you want.

When you reach the top of the pole, use an uninflated 260 to tie the 36" star onto the top of the column. Crisscross the 260 around and under the top few layers of balloons and tie.

To See The Companion Video Go To:
https://youtu.be/eKWyL5S9yh0

Star Arch

Materials:

- Balloon Arch Frame
- 200 11" balloons inflated to 8" (best to use 4 colors)

Always put a balloon cover on any exposed cut metal.

Take two duplets and twist them together into a quad with one balloon of each of your four colors.

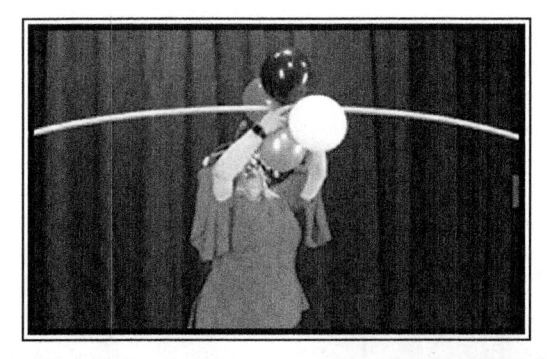

Wrap your first quad onto the arch at the center. Twist the balloons around each other to secure.

Pack the arch moving from the center out. Make sure you maintain the color order of your quads as you pack.

Spiral the colors in one direction for seven quads, and then reverse the spiral for the next seven. Continue changing spiral direction every seven quads until one side of the arch is filled.

When you begin working on the opposite side of the arch start with the opposite direction spiral for seven packs, and then reverse again for seven. Continue the pattern, alternating the spiral direction every seven quads, until the arch is completely filled.

It is helpful for this pattern to have a spotter to make sure you are maintaining the pattern.

To See The Companion Video Go To:
https://youtu.be/1qhkrCHLohY

Golden Awards Statue

Materials:
- Base plate and 7' pole
- 18 black 11" balloons
- 70 11" gold balloons
- 14 5" gold balloons
- 3 16" gold balloons
- Gold 260

RECIPE

Here is the cluster pattern starting from the bottom. Unless otherwise noted, all layers are **6-packs.**

1. BLACK 11" balloons sized to 9.5"
2. BLACK 11" balloons sized to 9.5"
3. BLACK 11" balloons sized to 9.5"
4. GOLD *2* 11" balloons sized to 9", *4* 5" balloons sized to 3.5"
5. GOLD *4-pack* 5" balloons sized to 3.5"
6. GOLD 11" balloons sized to 5"
7. GOLD 11" balloons sized to 5.5"
8. GOLD 11" balloons sized to 6"
9. GOLD *2* 11" balloons sized to 7.5", *4* 11" balloons sized to 6"
10. GOLD 11" balloons sized to 6.5"
11. GOLD *2* 11" balloons sized to 8.5", *4* 11" balloons sized to 6.5"
12. GOLD 11" balloons sized to 6.5"
13. GOLD *2* 11" balloons sized to 9", *4* 11" balloons sized to 6.5"
14. GOLD 11" balloons sized to 6.5"
15. GOLD *2* 16" balloons sized to 10.5", *4* 11" balloons sized to 6.5"
16. GOLD 11" balloons sized to 6.5"
17. GOLD 5" balloons sized to 3.5"
18. GOLD 16" SINGLE Balloon sized to 15"
19. * 2 11" balloons sized to 7.5" individually tied

This design is a little tricky as it uses multiple sizes of balloons, sometime in the same cluster. Pay attention to the details. It may be easier to follow with the video at

https://youtu.be/lqk3KJOvAoO

This design is based on a six pack of balloons. Tie two balloons together to create a duplet. Twist together two duplets to make a quad. For a six pack, twist in a third duplet.

Begin by wrapping a 9.5" black six pack at the base of the pole. Wrap two more six packs of the same size and color above the first. This is your statue base.

www.DiyBalloonArt.com

Take a 9" gold duplet and wrap it around the pole so that the balloons are next to each other in the front. These are the feet.

Wrap a 3.5" gold *quad* onto the pole behind the feet. Arrange so that all four are behind the two 9.5" balloons. Wrap a second 3.5" *quad* on top of the first. This builds the layer up so that it is level and ready for the next layer.

Wrap a six pack of 11" balloons sized to 5" on top of the feet balloons.

You are going to be incrementally increasing in size for each of the next few layers to create the legs. Continue for 2 more layers, going up ½" in each layer.

Next, create a six pack with four 6" gold balloons and two 7.5" gold balloons. Wrap the six pack around the pole and arrange so that the larger balloons are on the sides.

The next six pack is all 6.5" balloons. Wrap onto the pole.

Create a six pack with four 6.5" balloons and two 8.5" balloons. Wrap onto the pole so that the 8.5" balloons are on the sides, directly above the first set from the odd sized six pack.

Wrap a six pack of 6.5" balloons onto the pole.

Create a six pack with four 6.5" balloons and two 16" balloons sized to 10.5" balloons. Wrap onto the pole so that the larger balloons are on the sides.

Wrap a 6.5" six pack onto the pole.

Wrap a six pack of 5" balloons sized to 3.5" onto the top of the pole. This is a collar to hold the head stable.

Tie an uninflated 260 to the nozzle of a 16" balloons sized to 15. Use the 260 to tie the balloon to the top of the column. Tie below the second or third layer of six packs.

Tie half of a 260 to the nozzle of one 7.5" balloon. Tie the other end to the second 7.5" balloon.

Stretch the 260 and work into the statue below the second six pack at the top so that one balloon is on each side. This creates an epaulet look for the shoulders.

The DIY Balloon Bible Themes & Dreams

To See The Companion Video Go To:
https://youtu.be/Iqk3KJOvAo0

www.DiyBalloonArt.com

Hollywood Theme Photo Op Station

Materials:
- Photo Frame base
- 2 lamp bases 6' tall
- 2 pieces ½" PVC 5'
- 2 pvc "elbow" connectors ½"
- 2 pvc "t" connectors ½"
- Lots of packing or duck tape
- uninflated 260 balloons
- 168 5" round balloons, in quads, white
- 100 5" round balloons, in quads, black
- Mylar balloons, Hollywood theme
- Sticky tabs

To create a garland for easy packing of your frame, start by tying together two uninflated 260s. Tie a quad of 5" balloons onto the end of the two 260s.

The DIY Balloon Bible Themes & Dreams

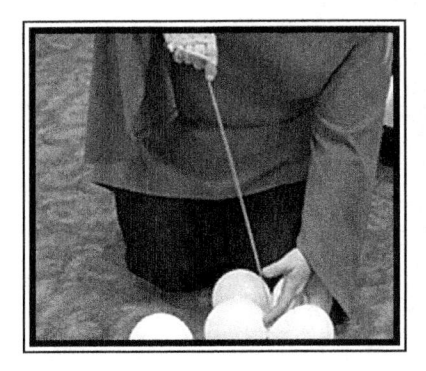

Wrap the uninflated 260s around your hand and hold so that the balloon string is taut. Place the quad on the ground to create counterpressure. Place a second quad on top of the first and figure-eight the 260s around the quad to secure.

Continue in this manner to pack your garland.

Make four garlands, one for each side of your photo frame.

The pattern for the Hollywood frame is one black quad, three white quads. You want something reminiscent of a film strip.

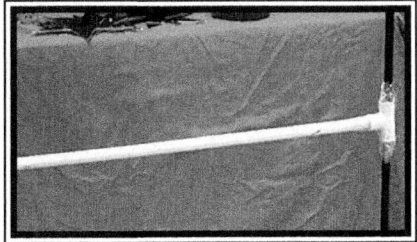

www.DiyBalloonArt.com 59

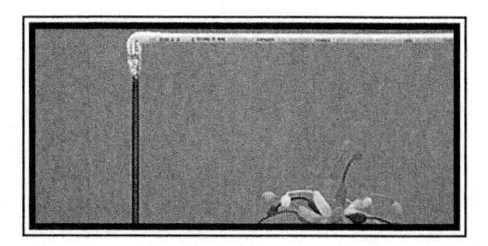

The photo frame is created with ½" PVC in two 5' lengths, two T connectors, two elbow connectors, and two lamp bases. This is an indoor frame. If you need an outdoor frame or something for a high traffic area use a 2x2' base plate and ½" poles and ¾" PVC.

To pack the frame, take a garland, open it up, and gently pull it onto the frame so that the pole runs in the center.

Use pieces of uninflated 260 to tie around the garland and secure the balloons to the frame.

The DIY Balloon Bible Themes & Dreams

Pack each side of the frame with a garland.

www.DiyBalloonArt.com

For the corners of the frame, use duplets and/or quads of black balloons to fill in the empty spaces and hide the pole. You can tie them in or twist them around the pole.

Use sticky tabs to attach Mylar balloons to the frame, along with any other embellishments you want.

Use the embellishments to hide any holes or other flaws.

To See The Companion Video Go To:
https://youtu.be/fg0zF_ynQeg

Candyland Theme

Balloon Candy

Materials:
- 5" round balloon
- Opalescent cellophane
  Ribbon

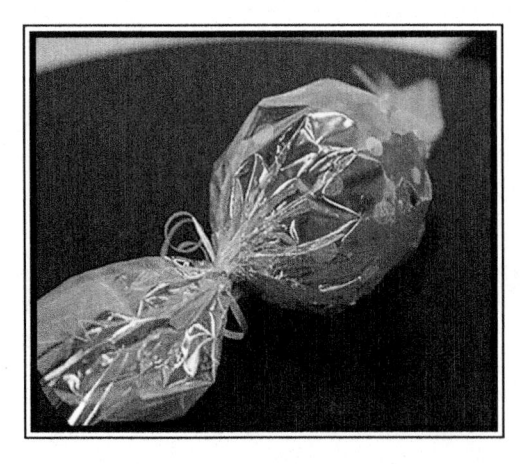

Inflate the 5" round balloon and tie off. Cut the nozzle off.

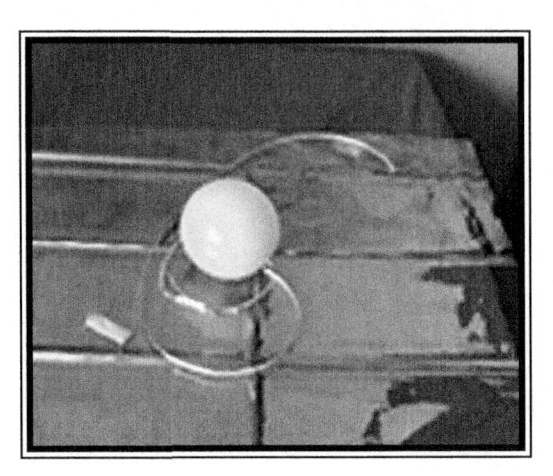

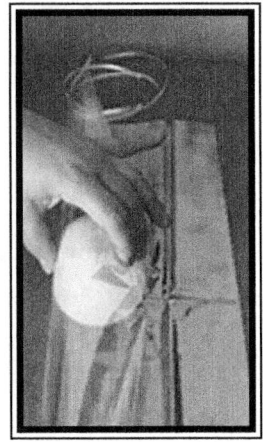

Roll the inflated balloon into the cellophane, so that you are wrapping the cellophane around the balloon. You may want to secure the cellophane with a small piece of tape.

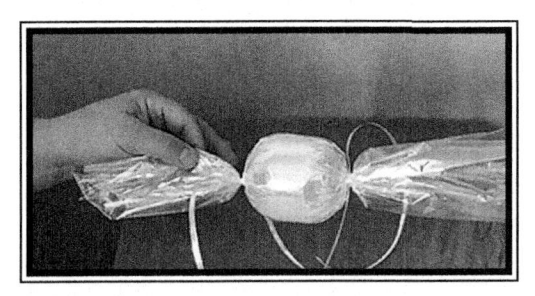

Gather one open end of cellophane and secure it with ribbon. Do the same to the other side.

Different shaped balloons will make different shaped candies.

To See The Companion Video Go To:
https://youtu.be/Ti9kDuVOR7Y

Balloon Lollipop

Materials:
- 4 260 balloons, partially inflated
- Sticky tabs if needed

Take a 260 balloon. Twist a small bubble.

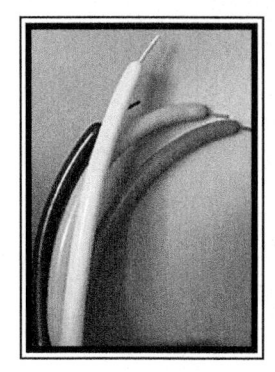

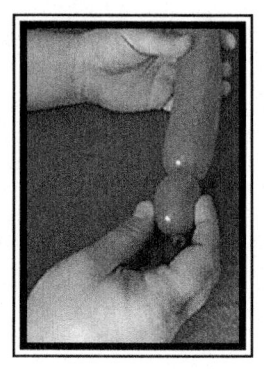

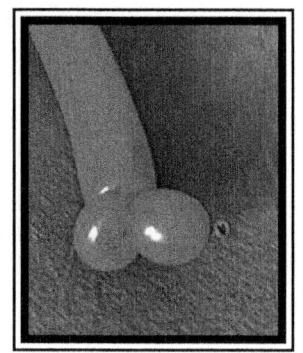

www.DiyBalloonArt.com

Make a small loop, securing with the bubble. Push the bubble through the center of the loop to further secure. Cut the nozzle off.

Make a small pinch twist by making a bubble and folding it in on itself by pulling up and twisting around. It looks like a bean or an ear.

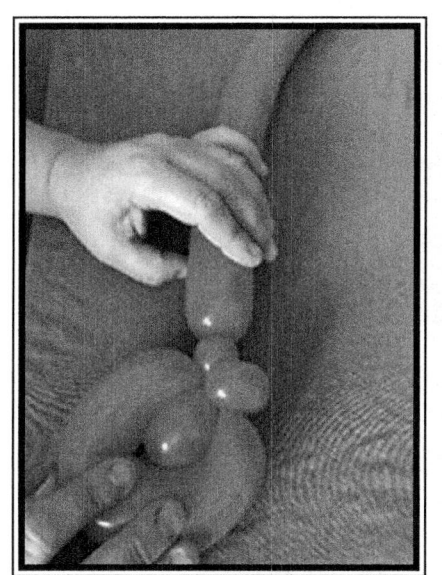

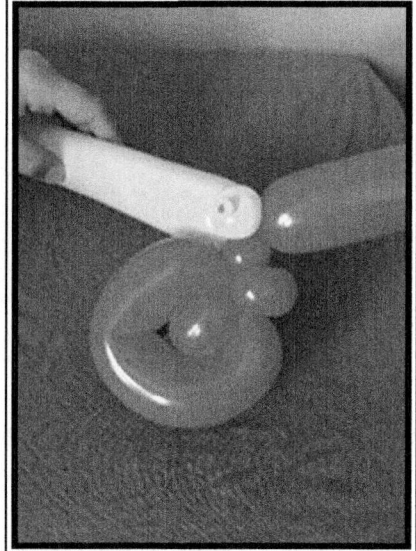

Twist a tiny bubble. Take a second 260 and twist a tiny bubble at the end. Wrap the two bubbles together to attach the second 260 to the first.

Wrap the second 260 around the first loop that you made. Twist the two 260s together to secure.

Make a pinch twist in the second 260. Make a second pinch twist with the nozzle end of the second 260.

Remove the excess of the first 260.

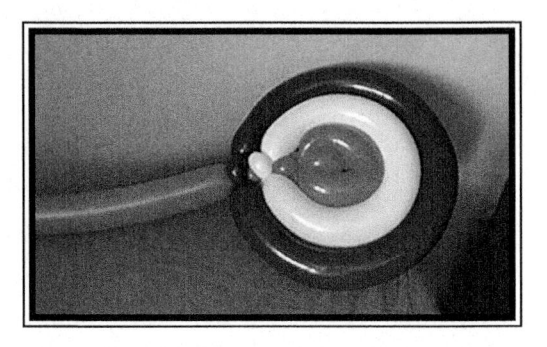

You are now going to add in another 260. Make a tiny bubble in the second 260. Make a tiny bubble at the end of a third 260, and wrap the two bubbles together to join.

Wrap the third 260 around the loop make by the first and second 260s. Twist the 260s together to secure.

Make two pinch twists in the third 260. Remove the excess of both the second and third 260s. Use sticky tabs in between the loops to secure them. Now you have the head of your lollipop.

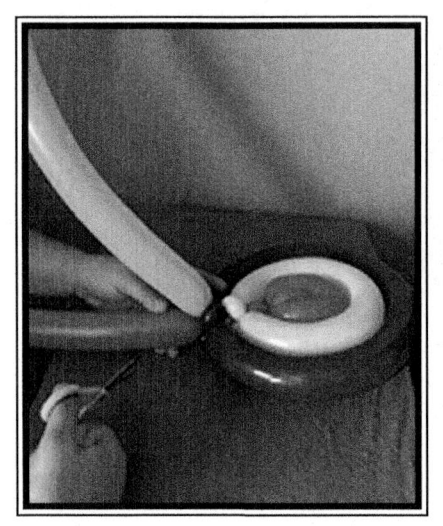

Take your last 260 and twist it into the bubbles on the outer ring. Wrap the twist into the pinch twists you made with the third 260.

Measure how long you want the "stick", twist it and hold onto it while you deflate the extra and tie off the the ends.

To See The Companion Video Go To:
https://youtu.be/uB7bUVlHIA8

Candy Tower

Materials:
- Standard balloon column in solid color topped with 3" round
- Balloon Candy
- Stiky tabs
- Scrap 260 balloons, about 3" long, inflated and tied off

Start with a standard column in any solid color, white or pink are my personal faves. The top balloon should either be a candy themed mylar balloon, a jumbo agate 30" balloon (as pictured), or any other bright colored balloon.

Use sticky tabs to stick candy onto the balloon column. Place candy all the way around the column.

Use scrap 260 balloons as sprinkles.

To See The Companion Video Go To:
ttps://youtu.be/-SrtP8hK4Uk

Giant Candy Cane

Materials:
- Lamp base (indoor only)
- 5' ¼" Aluminum rod
- 100 Duplets, red
- 100 Duplets, white

Take your aluminum rod and cover the ends with some tape to cover sharp edges. This will be covered by balloons.

Tape the aluminum rod to the lamp pole about half way up. Then give the top half of the aluminum rod above the pole a gentle bend to make the curve of your candy cane.

Twist red and white duplets together to make quads.

Wrap a quad onto the base of the pole with the white balloons next to each other and the red balloons next to each other. Do the same with the next quad, shifting so that the colors slowly start to spiral up the pole. Continue the pattern up the pole.

If you want to make a fast spiral, alternate the red and white balloons in each quad, rather than having the colors paired next to each other.

When you get to the aluminum rod only it is a little bit harder. It moves around when you try to wrap the quads on. Continue the spiral pattern of your quads up to the curve.

When you reach the curve you may need to wrap on a duplet and then a quad, because otherwise it may gap.

When you get to the end of the aluminum, you may want to tie a single balloon on the end if you cannot fit another quad on the end.

To See The Companion Video Go To:
https://youtu.be/wcoETx6aCcA

Gumball Machine

By John Justice

Materials:

- 260 multi colored balloon bubbles or pom poms
- 5" clear balloon

Inflate a 260 balloon half way. Twist a small bubble. Make a loop twist, about two or three fingers in size. Repeat six or seven times. Arrange the loops to sit flat. This is the base of your gumball machine.

Make some little balloon balls from pieces of different colored 260s. You can also use pomp oms instead of balloon balls.

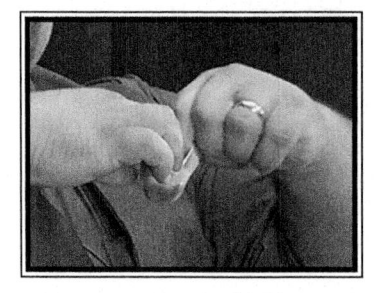

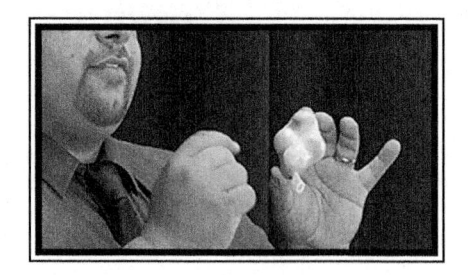

Take your 5" clear balloon and open up the nozzle with your fingers so that you are holding the balloon open. Stuff the balls that you made into the clear balloon.

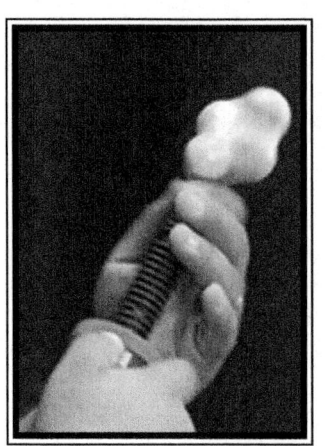

Use a pump to inflate the clear balloon. Grab the entire nozzle to give your clear balloon a round shape and tie off.

Wrap the nozzle of the clear balloon into the base that you made earlier to secure.

Take another 260. Put in a puff of air and wrap the nozzle into the base.

Sandi Masori, CBA

Measure around the wrist of the person who will wear the bracelet, and wrap the other end into the base. You can either remove the excess or hide it in the base.

John Justice, from Splendid Balloons is an award winning entertainer and decorator in the Colton, Ca area. You can find out more about him at http://www.SplendidBalloons.com .

To See The Companion Video Go To:
https://youtu.be/AXOk7PZQDFU

Giant Milkshake Balloon Sculpture

Materials:
- Base plate and pole
- 6- 16" silver balloons
- 6- 11" silver balloons
- 30- 11" pink balloons
- 18- 16" pink balloons
- 12- 16" white balloons
- 1 - 11" red balloon
- 9-15 – 5" white balloons
- 1 260 red balloon inflated ¾
- Uninflated 260s

RECIPE

Recipe order from bottom – NOTE this design is based on a SIX pack, that means every cluster has 6 balloons in it, unless otherwise noted.

1. 16" silver inflated to 10"
2. 11" silver inflated to 6"
3. 11" pink inflated to 5.5"
4. 11" pink inflated to 5"
5. 11" pink inflated to 5.5"
6. 11" pink inflated to 6"
7. 11" pink inflated to 7.5"
8. 11" pink inflated to 8"
9. 11" pink inflated to 9"
10. 11" pink inflated to 9.5"
11. 16" pink inflated to 10"
12. 16" white inflated to 10.5"
13. 16" white inflated to 9.5"
14. 11" white inflated to 7.25"
15. 11" red single balloon inflated to 9"

Then take some 5" white and tie them into clusters. This should be more organic with the number and size that looks best.

This design is based on a six pack. This is made by first creating a quad, by twisting together two duplets. Twist in a third duplet to create the six pack.

Start with a six pack of silver 16" balloons sized to 10" (width). Wrap the six pack onto the bottom of the pole. When you get it flattened out, make sure that you twist a few balloons to secure it.

Wrap the next silver six pack above the 10" balloons.

Next wrap on the first six pack of pink balloons. The sizes go up incrementally. Refer to the recipe at the top of the page for the sizes.

The largest size for the pink is going to go back up to 16" balloons. Even though the size by width appears to be the same in the recipe, the presence of the balloons is larger.

Next wrap on the first white cluster, this is also 16" balloons.

The last six pack goes back to 11" white balloons, wrapped at the very top of the pole.

Tie an uninflated 260 to the red balloon and use it to the tie the balloon to the very top of your column as a cherry.

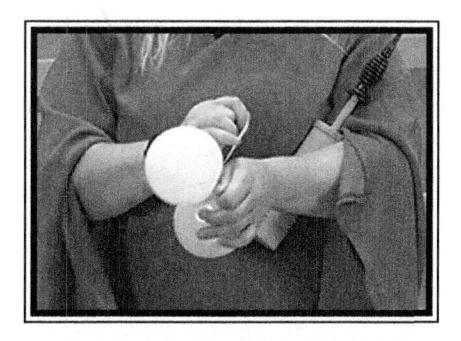

The randomly sized 5" white balloons will be your drips of whip cream. Tie into groups of three and fours.

Use an uninflated 260 to tie together two groups of 5" white balloons to make a small cluster. Place the cluster on your column where desired, and use the 260 to tie it to the pole.

Tie an uninflated 260 to another group of 5" balloons. Tie the other end of the 260 to a second cluster.

Wrap the 260 around the first cluster of 5" balloons you tied to the pole. Arrange into the shape you want.

Add more 5" balloons for more drips if desired

Take the red 260 and work it into the white six packs at the top of the column. This is your straw.

To See The Companion Video Go To:
https://youtu.be/OgiuL-vxtsc

Out-of-This World Theme

Astronaut

Materials:

- One 5" Balloon, Face print
- One 5" Balloon, Clear
- Two 260 balloons, white, inflated with 2" tail and burped
- Three 160 balloon, yellow, inflated with tail

First you are going to stuff the face print balloon into the clear balloon. Fold the face print balloon in on itself. Place the folded balloon into the clear balloon.

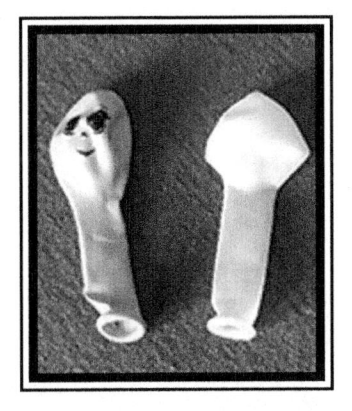

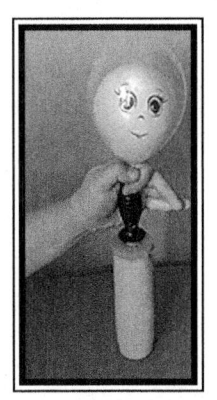

Inflate the inside balloon slightly. Hold the inside balloon nozzle closed while inflating the clear balloon more. Tie both balloons together.

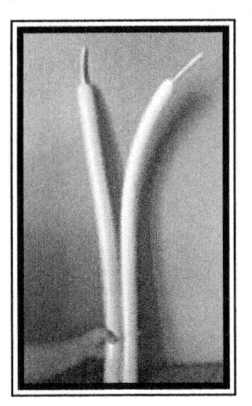

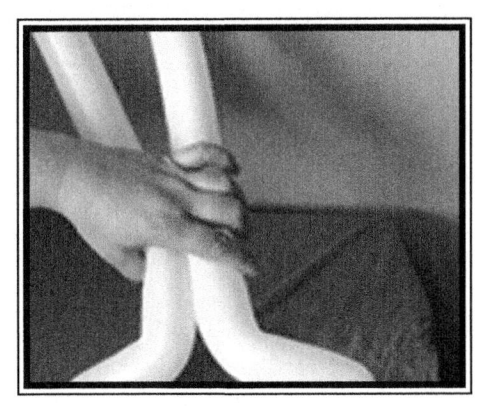

Take two white 260s. Make a bend a few inches down on each balloon.

Hold the two 260s so that the "arms" are together. Grab a few inches below the elbow bend and twist the two balloons together.

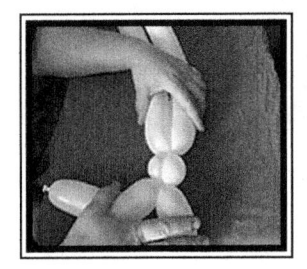

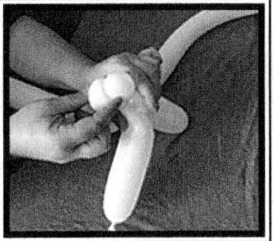

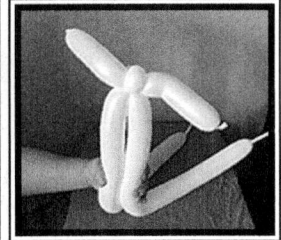

Make two pinch twists below the twist. Twist a small bubble in both balloon at the same time. Hold the bubbles together, pull up, and twist. Arrange so that there is one pinch twist on each side. This is the neck and will stabilize the head.

Grab an open handful of both balloons below the pinch twists and twist. Feed one 260 through the bubbles to secure.

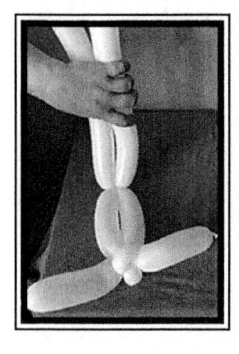

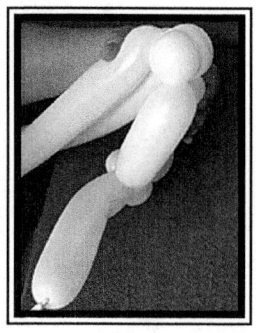

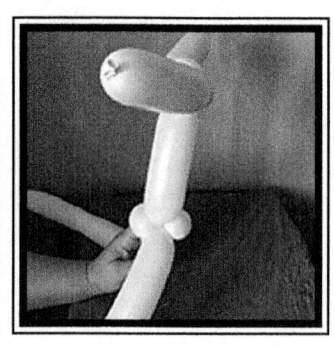

Make two small pinch twists to stabilize. Repeat what you did for the neck, but smaller. Put one on each side.

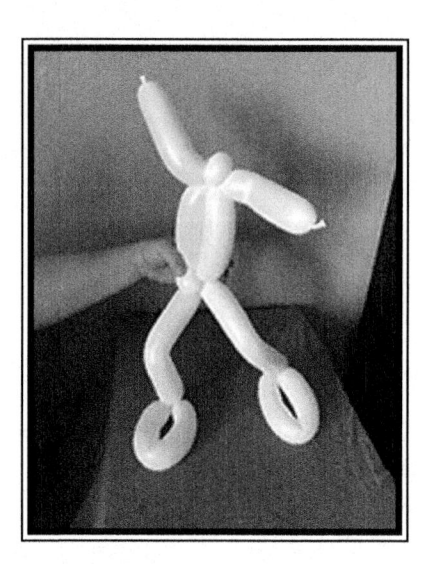

Give the remaining ends of the 260 a little stretch to lengthen. Bend a few inches from the small pinch twists to create a knee.

At the end of the 260, twist a small bubble. Make a small loop and twist. The size of the loop will depend on how much balloon is left at this point. Do the same on the second 260.

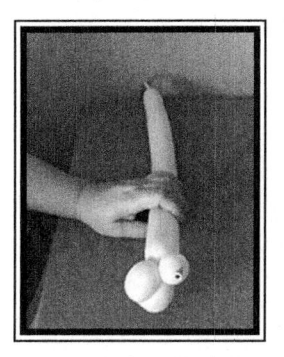

Take a third 260, the same color as the head, and make two small "dog legs" with a little bubble. Tie them off and set aside.

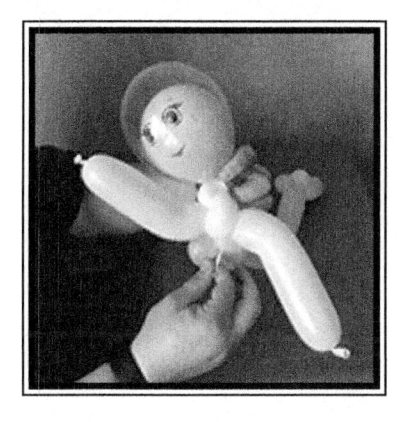

Take the nozzle of the head balloon and wrap it into the neck pinch twists. Tuck the nozzle into the body when secure.

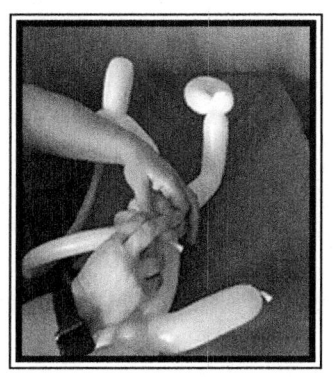

Take the yellow 160 and wrap it around the waist and twist. This is the belt. Use the nozzle to join the gold 160. Wrap the nozzle into the waist pinch twists to secure. Put two three small pinch twists into the gold balloon.

Squeeze the air in the remaining part of the 160 to stretch it. Wrap the end of the 160 around your hand to create a spiral. This is the leash that tethers the astronaut to the spaceship.

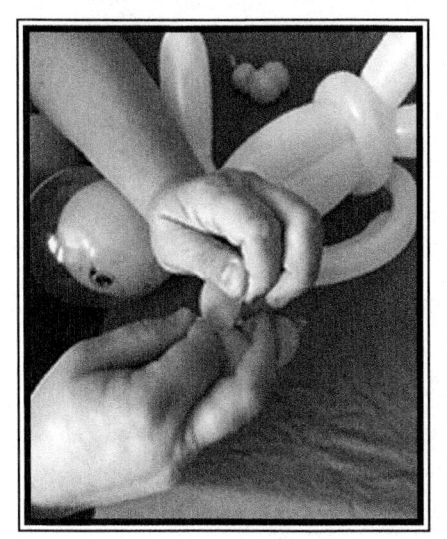

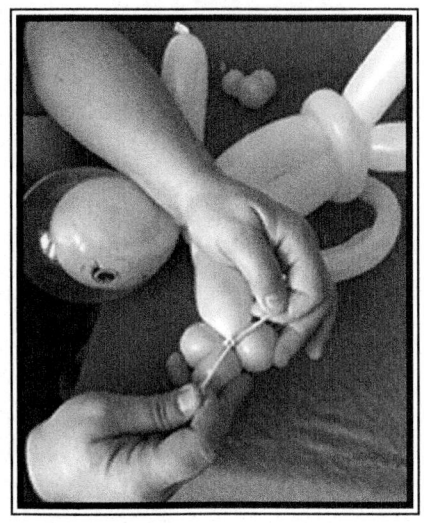

Tie in the little "dog heads" using the nozzles of the white balloon.

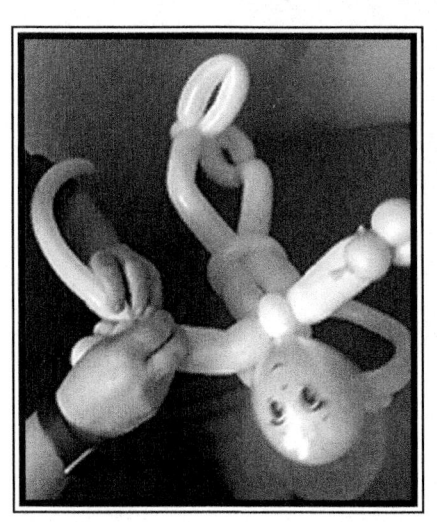

Take another yellow 160. Stretch. Wrap the 160 around the wrist and tie. Remove excess without deflating and tie off. Repeat the same process on the other wrist and both ankles.

Take a third gold 160. Twist a small bubble at the end and wrap into the pinch twist at the neck. Wrap around the neck. Bring the 160 up and around the head. Tie off and remove excess.

Play with different color combinations for different looks. J

To See The Companion Video Go To:
https://youtu.be/cVx0uz7iYJo

Twisted Rocket Ship

Materials:
- 260 balloon, fully inflated and burped
- 260 balloon, inflated with a 2" tail
- 260 balloon, inflated with a tail and burped.

Squeeze air down slightly from the end of the fully inflated 260 so that you can tie it to the nozzle, creating a circle.

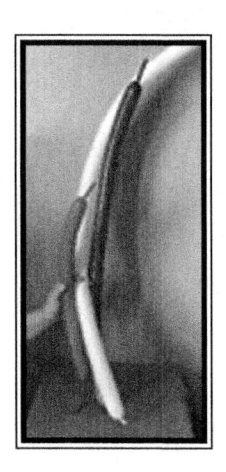

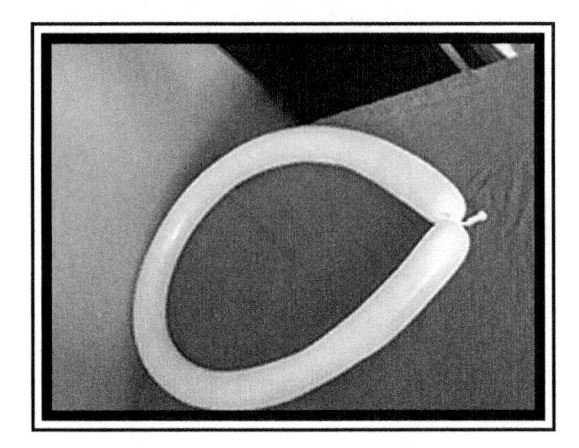

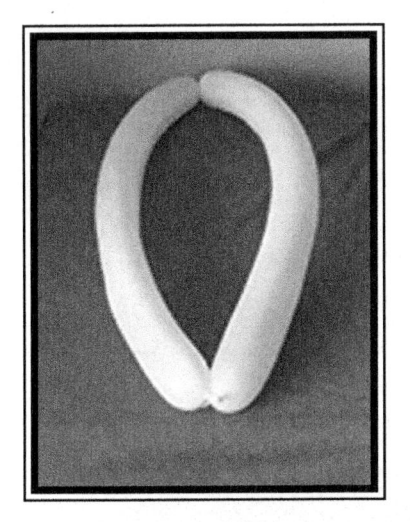

While holding the tied end of the 260 grab directly across from it with your other hand, pinch to divide the circle into two halves. While pinching, rotate one side.

Fold in half to find the center point and twist. You should have something that looks like a figure eight.

Fold at the twist you just made. You have four equal long bubbles. Rotate one bubble over the other. This creates a football shape. You can also wrap the nozzle around the connections.

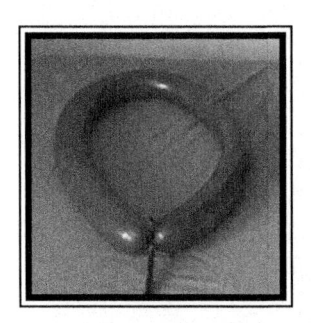

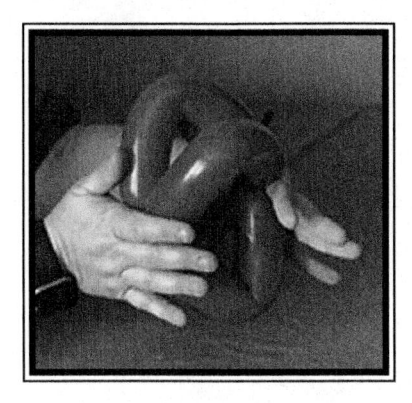

Take the partially inflated 260 and tie it into a circle. Repeat the steps you did with the first balloon up to the point of making a figure eight shape and folding it in half.

While holding each end of the folded figure eight, squish your hands together to flatten it and twist. It makes a four petal flower shape.

Measure about a third of the way from the center up one petal. Squeeze and twist to divide the petal into two bubbles, about 1/3 and 2/3 of its length. Do the same to all four.

With the twists you just made on the bottom, use the tail that you left on the 260 to tie into the first 260. Wrap around and through both 260s to secure. This is your rocket base and body.

If you want the rocket to really stand on its own, you could place a water weight into the bottom of the base.

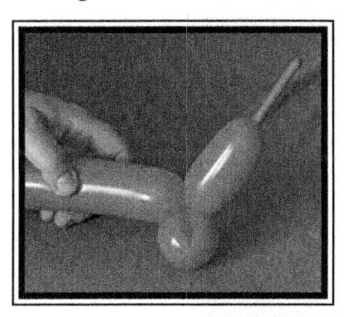

Take the third 260. Starting at the top of the 260, twist a small bubble.

Next twist three tiny loops. Remove the excess and figure eight around the loops to secure.

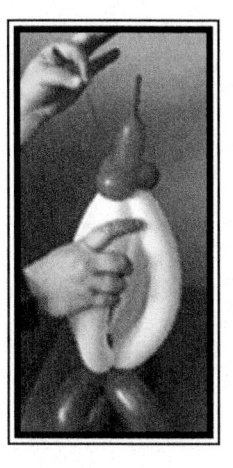

Use the deflated excess to tie onto the top of the rocket.

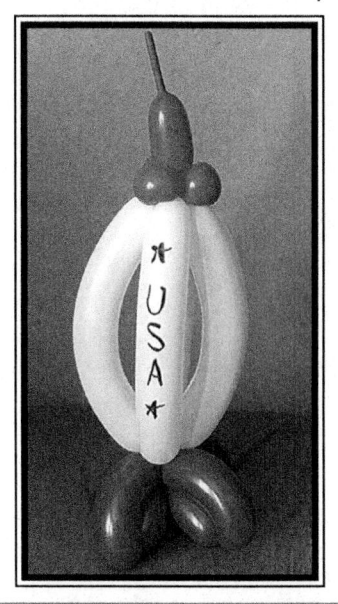

To See The Companion Video Go To:
https://youtu.be/fHl8Hwo9ppg

Ray Gun

By Darren Saari

Materials:

- Two 260 balloons, inflated with tail

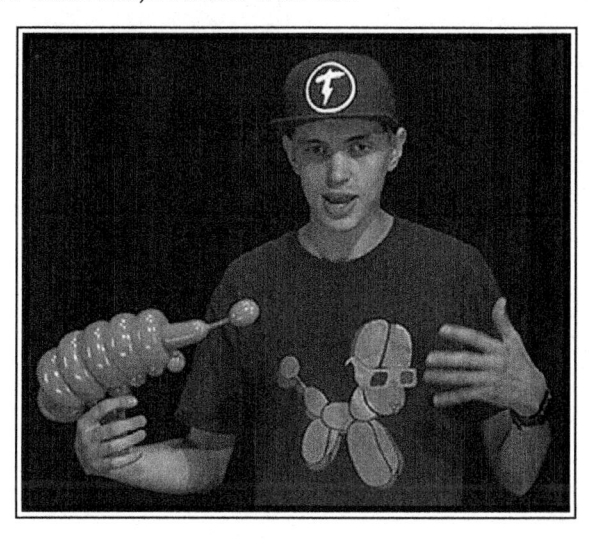

Take a 260 balloon and make a pinch twist. Make a loop that is big enough for a balloon to fit through, about five fingers. Twist.

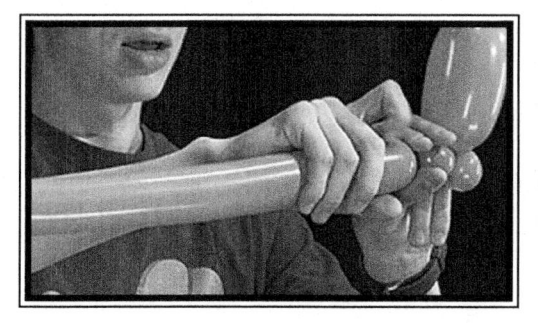

Twist a small bubble. Twist a loop slightly smaller than the first one.

Feed the 260 through the two loops you made.

Take the second 260. This will be the handle. Twist a bubble a few fingers long and twist into the pinch twist of the first balloon. Arrange so that the pinch twist is in front of the handle.

Twist a small bubble in the second balloon. Make a loop about the same size as the first loop and twist.

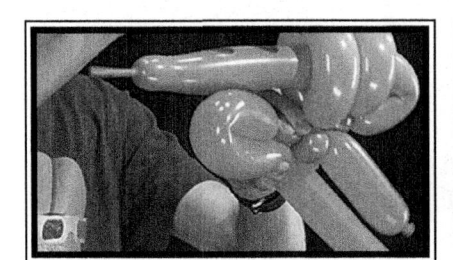

Twist a small bubble and a second slightly smaller loop.

Twist a third small bubble and smaller loop.

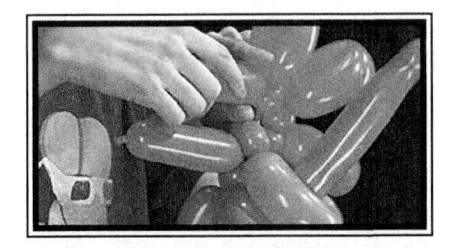

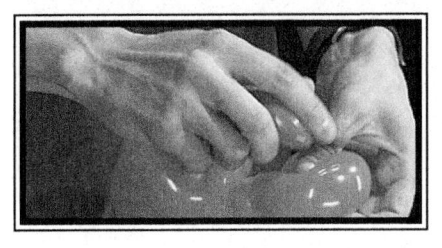

Make a small pinch twist. Remove the excess balloon and tie the end around the pinch twist.

Pull the remaining part of the first balloon through the three loops of the second balloon.

Pull some air to the end of the first balloon to make a bubble.

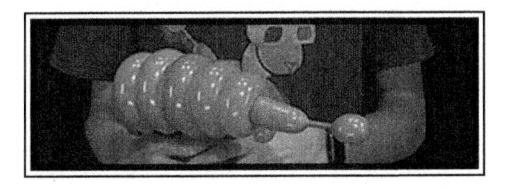

*Darren Saari, from TwiistBalloons is an up and coming balloon artist from the Moreno Valley area. To learn more about Darren, or to book him for an event go to http://www.TwiistBalloons.com

To See The Companion Video Go To:
https://youtu.be/HxtTRZtE8e8

Planets

Materials:

- 11" Agate balloons, inflated 9"
- 260 balloon, inflated with 1" tail
- 30" agate balloon, inflated 20-24"
  Two 350 balloons, inflated with 1" tail

Twist a small bubble at the end of the 260 and make a pinch twist. Make a second pinch twist the same size.

Wrap the pinch twists into the nozzle of the agate balloon.

Wrap the 260 around the agate balloon, wrap around the pinch twists, and make another pinch twist to secure.

To supersize the planet, take the 30" agate balloon. If it bounces without popping, it is inflated to a good size.

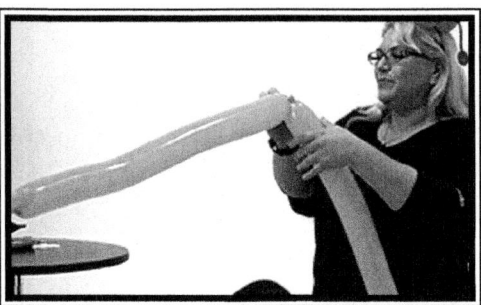

Tie the 350 balloons into a duplet. Put a pinch twist into each 350 at the ends by the knot.

Wrap the nozzle of the 30" agate into the pinch twists.

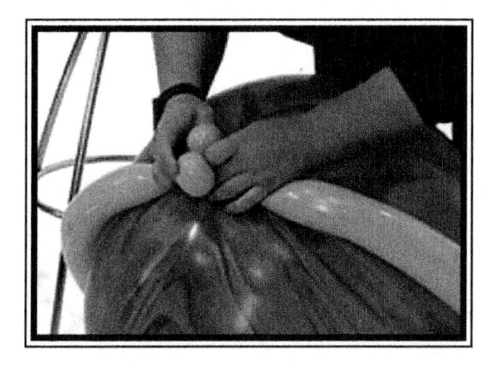

Squeeze the air down in the 350 balloons to get enough length to reach around the 30" balloon.

Twist bubbles on the ends of each 350 balloon. Wrap the 350s around the center of the 30" agate and twist the bubbles together.

To See The Companion Video Go To:
https://youtu.be/UQfiNWgrJfE

Twisted Star

Materials:
- 160 balloon

Inflate the 160 balloon, leaving a tail of about 6".

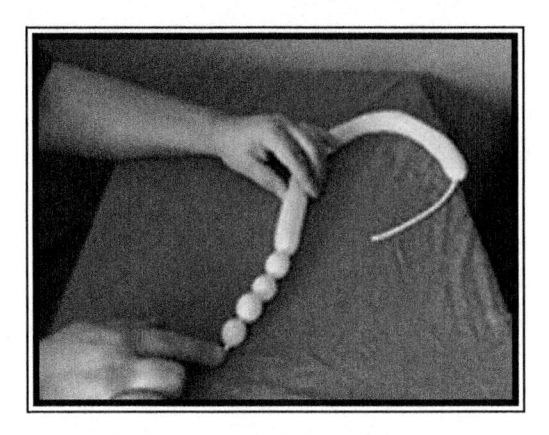

Make sure to control your bubbles as you twist, and make sure that all the bubbles are the same size.

Twist one bubble. As you continue, always twist in the same direction and the same number of times. Hold the first bubble with your pinkie, and twist the second bubble.

Continue twisting until you have a chain of four bubbles.

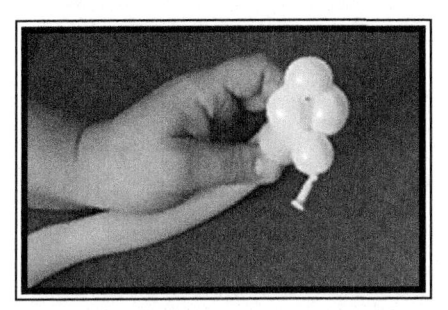

Twist the second and fourth bubbles together.

Do the same sequence five times. Twist four bubbles, and twist the second and fourth bubbles together.

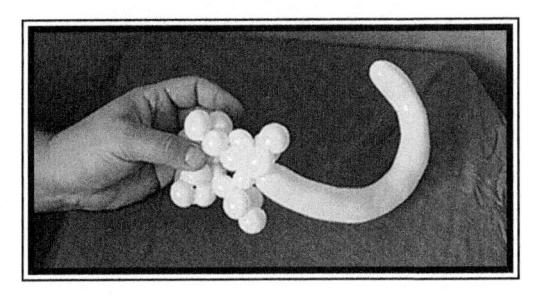

On the last set take the nozzle and tie it into the last set that you made. Wrap it around to secure.

You need to twist five more bubbles. Twist your bubble in the center and wrap it around one of the sets you made. Repeat for five bubbles. This will give you star more strength.

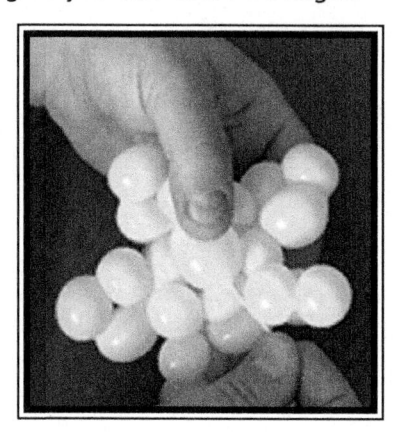

Deflate and remove the excess balloon.

If you don't want the hole in the center you could make a last bubble and tie it in the center.

Arrange your points to make your star shape.

To See The Companion Video Go To:
https://youtu.be/pXf4giSUYEY

Alien Airplane

Materials:
- Four 350 balloons, fully inflated and burped
- One 350 balloon, inflated with a 3" tail
- One 260 balloon, fully inflated and burped
- Printed head balloon or round with face drawn on

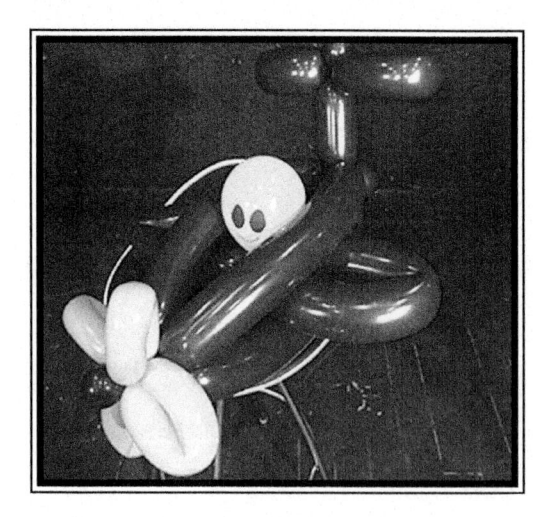

Take a fully inflated 350. Twist a bubble on the nipple end. Take the nozzle of the balloon and wrap it around the bubble.

Find the center across from the bubble. Pinch and twist one side of the 350 a few times.

Do the same thing with a second 350 balloon.

Hold the two 350s one on top of the other, with the bubbles on opposite sides. Wrap the bubble of one 350 around the twist in the other. Do the same on the other side.

Take a third fully inflated 350. Do the same as you did with the first two 350s. Twist a bubble. Wrap the nozzle around the bubble. Find the center. Pinch and twist.

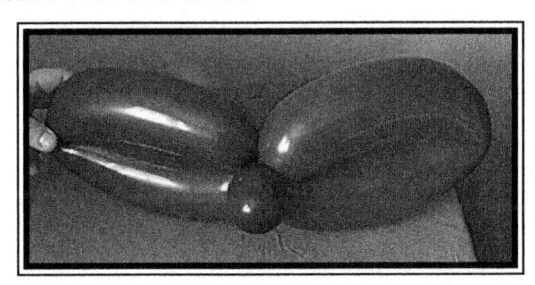

With one hand on the bubble and one hand on the twist, bring your hands together. Wrap the bubble around the twist a few times. You should have a figure eight shape. Flip the bubble through one of the loops to secure.

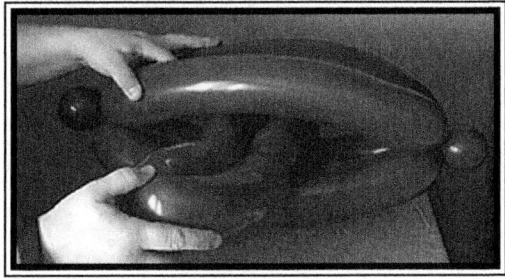

Insert the figure eight shape into the center of the first two 350s so that one half comes out on either side. These are your airplane wings.

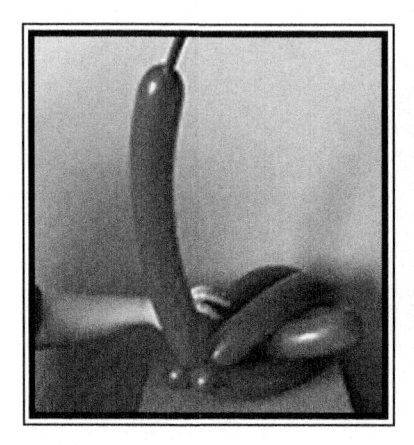

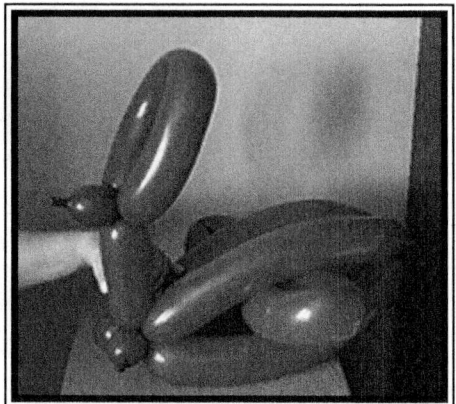

Take the partially inflated 350. Twist a bubble on the nipple end. Twist the bubble around one of the bubbles in the first two 350s. It doesn't matter which side.

Squeeze the air up. Measure up from the bubbles about a handful and twist.

Squeeze the air up to the end. Make a bubble at the end. Bring it down to the twist you made and wrap it around. Feed the bubble through the loop to secure.

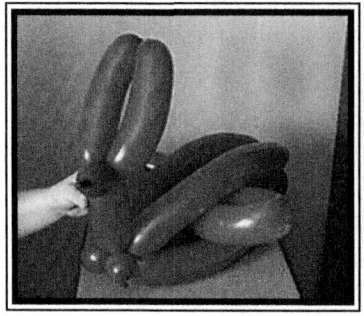

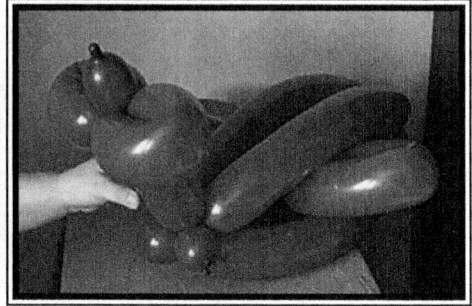

Find the center. Pinch and twist.

Squeeze to bring the twist in to the bubble that you made. Twist the bubble around to secure.

Take your head balloon and tie it into the center of the wings, inside the airplane.

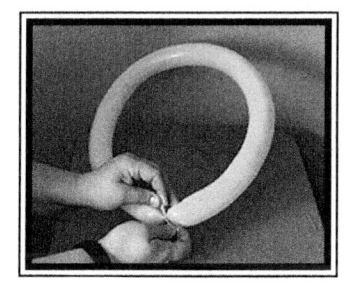

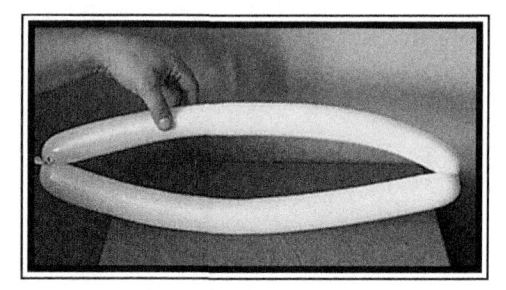

Take the 260 balloon. Stretch it a bit and tie it into a circle. Find the center across from the tie. Squeeze and twist.

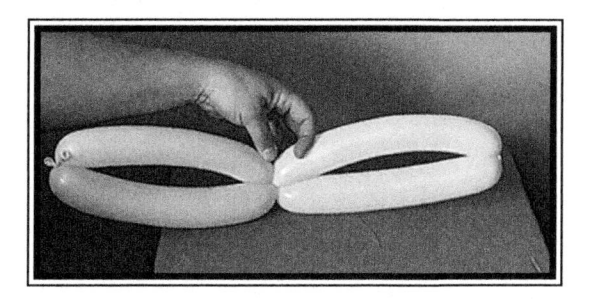

Fold the 260 in half. Squeeze and twist in the center. You have a figure eight shape.

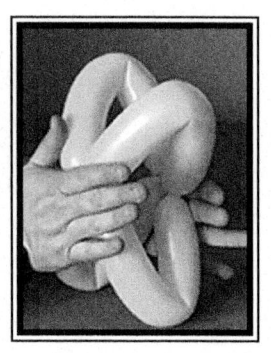

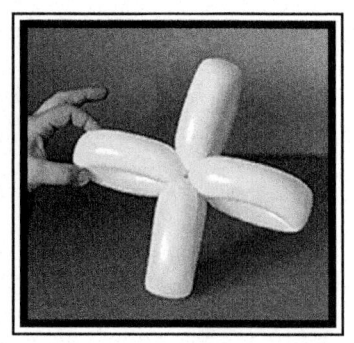

Fold the figure eight over into a football shape. Squish the sides together and twist in the middle. You have a four petal flower shape. This is your propeller.

Take the ball at the front of your airplane and wrap it around the center of the flower shape.

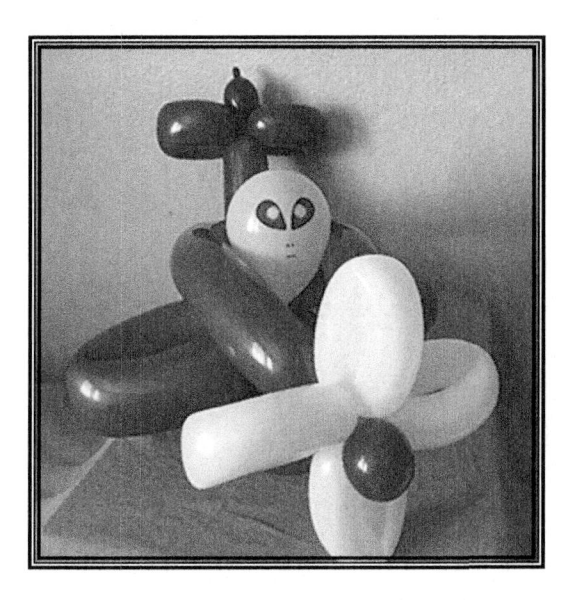

**To See The Companion Video Go To:
https://youtu.be/N7XjuC2eZyl**

Out-of-This World Photo Frame

Materials:
- Two base plates and poles
- Two 5' lengths ½" PVC
- Two PVC elbow connectors
- Two PVC T connectors
- Round balloons, packed in quads
- Uninflated 260s
- Foil star balloons
- Sticky tabs
- Balloon astronaut
  Balloon ray gun

First create the frame base. Attach T connectors to each end of one of the 5' lengths of PVC. Attach elbow connectors to each end of the second 5' length.

Slide the T connectors over the poles. Bring down to where you want the bottom of the frame and tape to the poles. Use more tape than you think you need.

Slide the elbow connectors onto the top of each pole and secure with tape.

Create balloon garlands to fit the four sides of the frame. Tie together two uninflated 260 balloons.

Take the nozzle end of the two uninflated 260s and wrap around a quad in a figure-eight a few times to secure.

Wrap the remainder of the uninflated 260 around your hand to create tension. Lay a quad on top of the first and figure-eight around with the 260.

Continue adding quads and wrapping with 260 until you reach the size that you want.

To attach the garland to the frame, hold the garland on top of the pvc, separate the balloons and push down over the pipe. Repeat the length of the garland. To secure, use an uninflated 260 to tie the garland string to the pole in a few places.

Do the same thing with each of the four sides of the frame.

Use sticky tabs to attach foil stars to the balloons of the frame.

Attach balloon ray guns, planets, stars, astronaut or any other outer space embellishment that you fancy onto the frame with sticky tabs.

The DIY Balloon Bible Themes & Dreams

To See The Companion Video Go To:
https://youtu.be/BuwIkgn6SOo

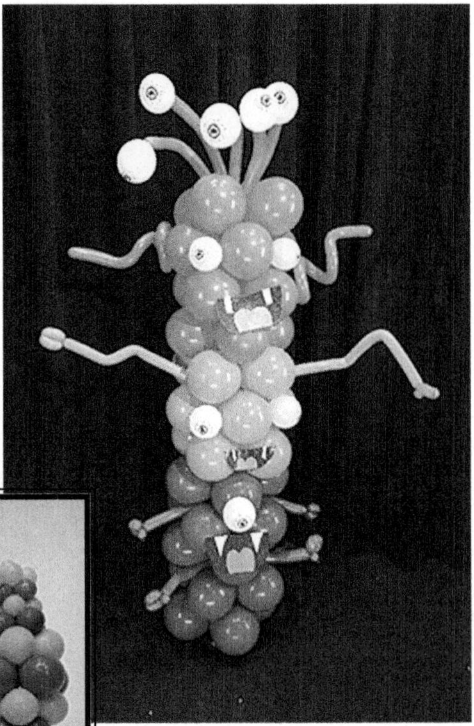

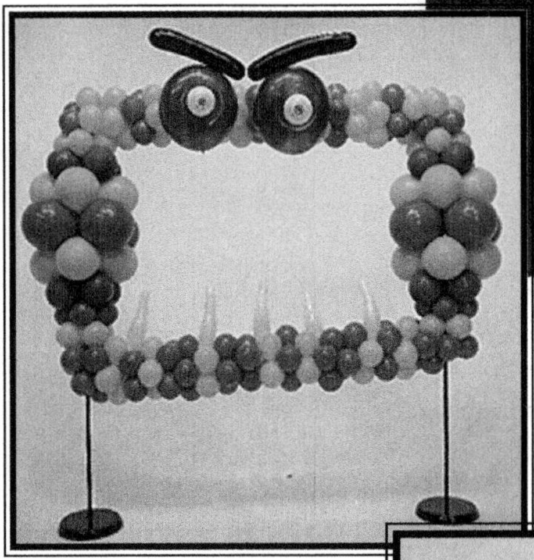

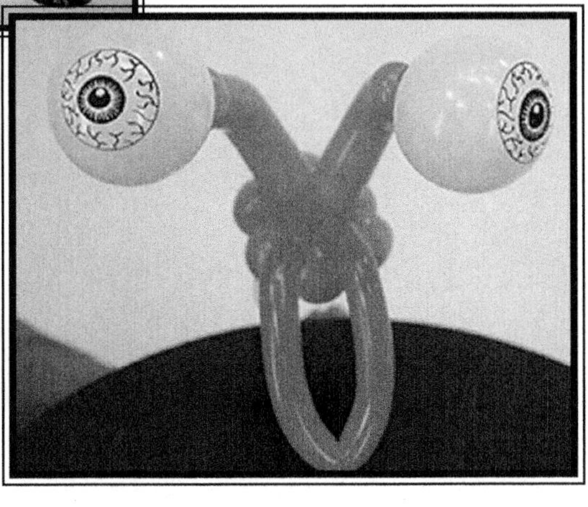

Monster Theme

Monster Headband

By Caity Byrne

Materials:
- Two 260 balloons, inflated with a tail
- Two 5" round eye balloons
- 160 balloon, partially inflated
- Headband

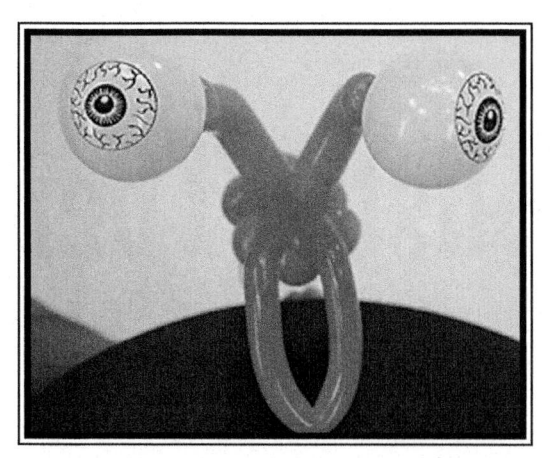

Begin by using a 260 to make a six petal flower. Make six small loops of the same size. Remove the excess and twist it into the flower.

Now you are going to make the eye stalks. Twist two equal sized bubbles at the end of a 260. Wrap them into themselves and tuck the nozzle through to secure. Pinch the two bubbles together and twist to make two pinch twists.

Come down about two inches and make a shock twist. Fold the balloon over and pull a piece of the latex hard. This shocks the balloon into bending.

Measure down a few inches from the bend. Twist and wrap into the middle of the six petal flower.

Bring the 260 up. You now want to match the first eye. Create your shock twist at the same height. Make two pinch twists. Remove the excess and tie off.

Take your eye balloons and wrap them into the pinch twists.

Tie the 160 into a circle. Remove the excess.

Place the 160 over the eye stalks and push it between the flower and the base of the eye stalks and over to the side. Bend and shape the tongue by squeezing.

Sandi Masori, CBA

Hold the headband at the bottom of the six petal flower with your thumb. Wrap the excess from the flower around the headband a few times to secure.

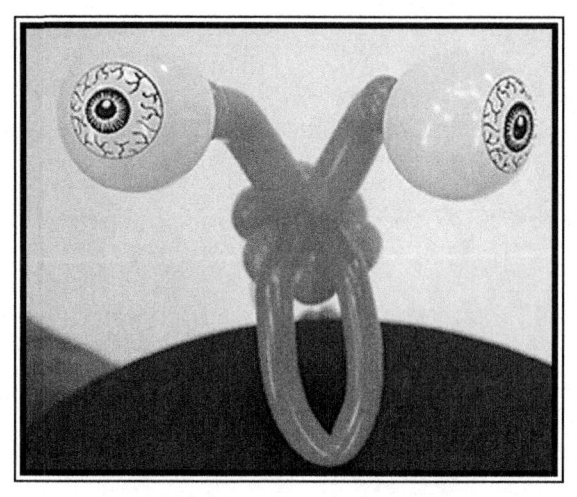

*Caity Byrne is the CEO of All About Balloons, a national balloon decoration company. For more information about Caity or All About Balloons, go to Http://www.AllAboutBalloons.com

To See The Companion Video Go To:
https://youtu.be/-L3AgHzMdYI

Monster Totem Pole

Materials:

- Base plate and pole
- 8" round balloons, twisted in quad
- round eye balloons
- glitter paper
- sticky tabs
- 260 balloons

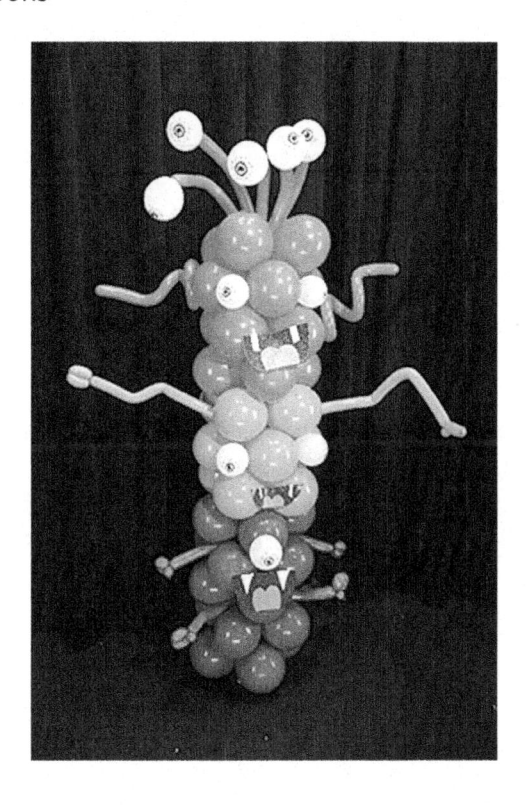

The great thing about the monster design is that there is no right or wrong. It's a great place to get creative and have fun with it. Get the kids to help too, they love getting to help decorate.

Wrap a quad around pole at the base. Pack a total of five quads of one color onto the pole.

Switch colors. Wrap three quads of the second color onto the pole.

Switch colors. Wrap quads in third color until you reach the top of the pole.

Cut an uninflated 260 in half. Tie a white eye balloon onto the end of one half. Tie the second eye balloon to the opposite end.

Wrap the eyes into the middle group of quads so that there is one on each side.

Make mouths out of glitter paper- like the kind that is used for scrapbooking. Be creative, since these are monsters, there's no right or wrong. Use sticky tabs to attach the mouth to the center group of quads where you would like it.

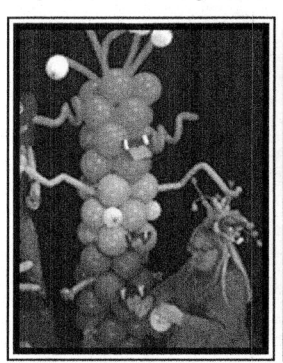

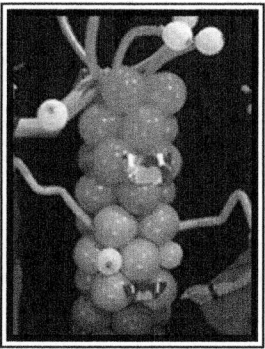

Tie together two 260 balloons. Twist a dog's head at each end to create two hands.

Wrap into the center quad so that one arm sticks out on either side. Bend balloons to give arms shape.

Tie an eye balloon onto each end of a 260. Repeat with two more 260s.

Wrap the 260s into the quad at the top of the column so that they stick up.

Use sticky tabs to place the mouth where you want on the top monster.

Twist a dog leg onto the end of a 260 to create a hand. Repeat with a second 260. Bend to give the arms shape. Twist the two arms into the bottom monster.

Feel free to be as creative as you like creating the monsters and adding eyes, arms, mouths, and/or hair. There is no wrong way to do it.

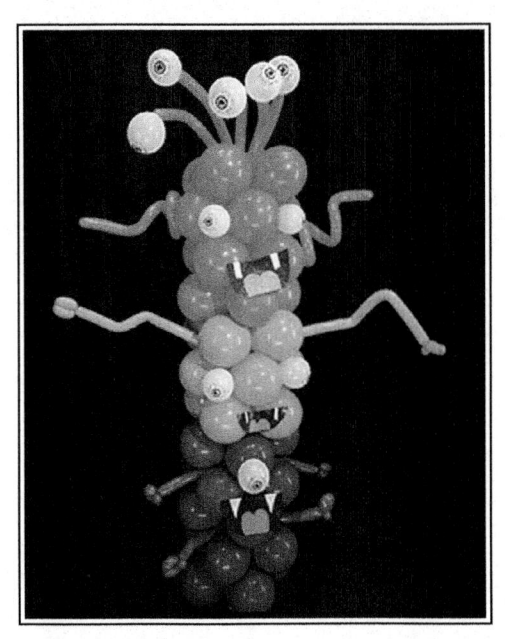

To See The Companion Video Go To:
https://youtu.be/aGaCE-grjuY

Monster Photo Frame

By Caity Byrne

Materials:

- Picture frame (2 Lamp Bases 6', 2 pieces of ½" pvc,
- 2 ½" elbow connectors, 2 ½" "T" connectors, lots of packing or duck tape)
- 8- 11" balloons sized to 9" tied in quads
- 8- 11" balloons sized to 7" tied in quads
- 8- 11" balloons sized to 6" tied in quads
- 200 - 5" balloons sized to 4" tied in quads
- 2- 16" geo donuts
- 2 - 5" eyeball print balloons
- 2- 350 balloons, partially inflated
- Glue dots
- 5- 321 balloons

Begin with a picture frame about five feet across.

Wrap a 9" quad in onto the side of the frame in the center. Wrap 7" quads above and below. Repeat on the opposite side.

Wrap 6" quads on top of the 7" quads. Do the same at the bottom. Repeat on the opposite side.

Pack the rest of the frame with 4" quads. You can also use duplets instead of quads to pack the frame if you find it easier.

Tie an uninflated 260 to each eyeball print. Feed the 260 through the geo donut. Use the 260 to attach the eyeball and geo donut to the top of the frame. Do the same with the second eyeball and geo donut.

To give the monster eyebrows use the two 350 balloons. Remove any excess and tie off. Attach the eyebrows above the eyes with glue dots.

Use 321 balloons for the teeth. You can use glue dots or uninflated 260s to attach the 321 to the bottom of the frame.

*Caity Byrne is the CEO of All About Balloons, a national balloon decoration company. To learn more about Caity or All About Balloons, visit Http://www.AllAboutBalloons.com

To See The Companion Video Go To:
https://youtu.be/wi7AiJxzHzU

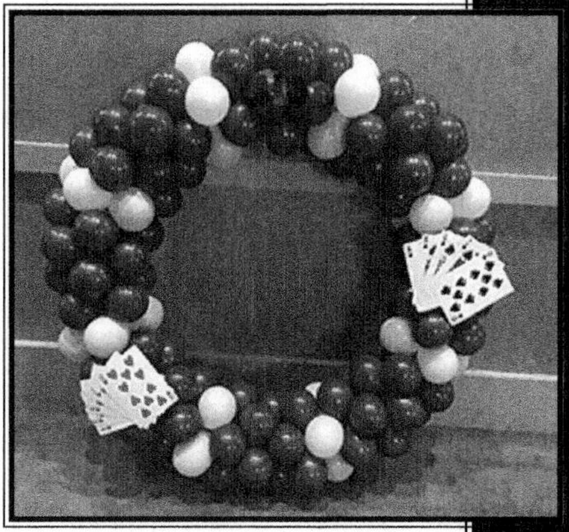

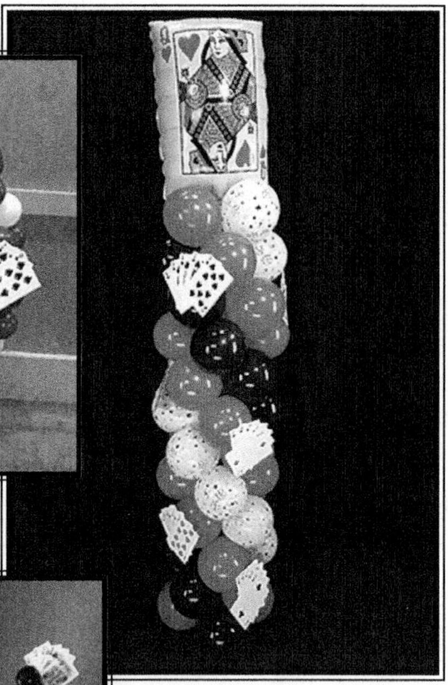

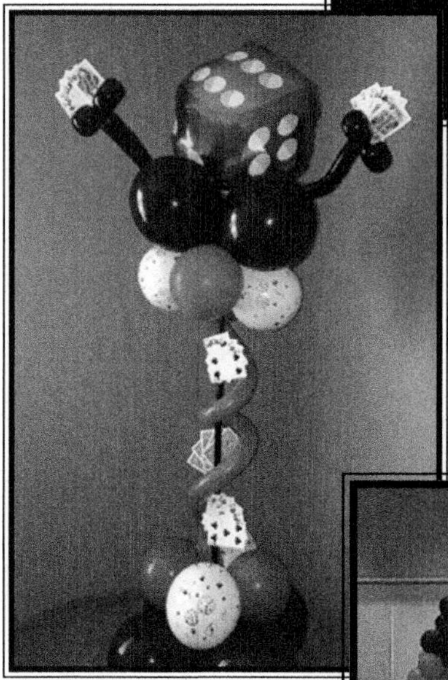

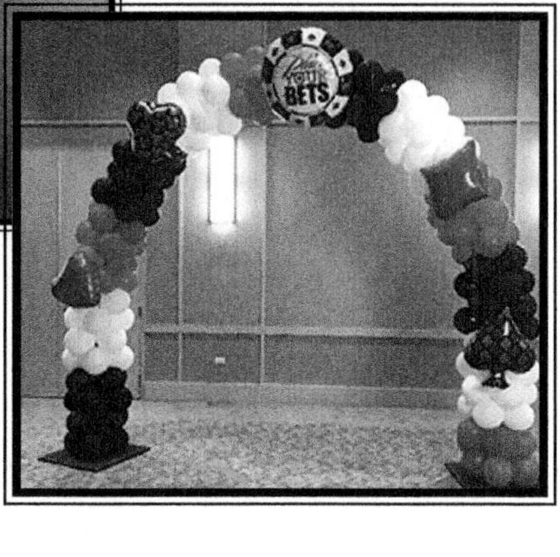
BETS

Casino Theme

Casino Tower

Materials:
- 6' Base plate and pole
- Large playing cards, taped in fans of five
- Sticky tabs
- 24 11" balloons, red, tied in duplets
- 12 11" balloons, cards around design
- 12 11" balloons, black
- Card foil balloon
- Uninflated 260 balloon

Tie card design balloons and black balloons into duplets with one of each.

Wrap together red duplets and black/card duplets into quads.

Wrap quad around the base of pole. Cross one balloon over another to secure. Arrange quad so that colors alternate, red, card, red, black.

Place a second quad on top of the first, making sure to continue pattern.

Continue wrapping quads up the pole, spiraling the colors as you go.

Sandi Masori, CBA

Tie an uninflated balloon onto the nozzle of the foil balloon, being careful not to tie around the valve. Use the 260 to secure the balloon to the top of the pole. Bring the 260 down in figure-eights around first few quads. Tie.

Make card fans using jumbo playing card. Use tape or sticky tabs to form them into poker hands. Use sticky tabs to place giant card fans onto column. Place them wherever looks good to you. Feel free to use other casino themed embellishments that you may find at the party store. It's all about being creative and adding extra elements to the standard column.

To See The Companion Video Go To:
https://youtu.be/keMlRSMz_5U

136 www.DiyBalloonArt.com

Poker Centerpiece

Materials:
- Base plate and pole
- Playing cards, taped into fans of winning hands
- Eight 11" balloons inflated to 7.5", black, quads
- Eight 11" balloons, red and cards around sized to 5", quads
- Die foil balloon
- Uninflated 260
- One 260 balloons, black, uninflated
- Three 260 balloons, black, inflated half way

Wrap an 7.5" quad around the base of the pole.

Wrap a 5" quad above the 7.5".

Mirror the bottom at the top of the pole. Wrap a 7.5" quad on top, with a 5" quad below it.

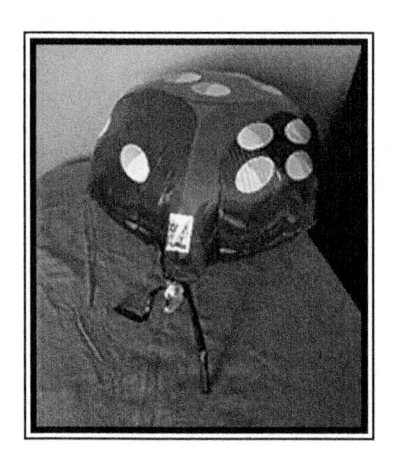

Tie an uninflated 260 the nozzle of the air-filled die balloon. Use the 260 to secure the foil balloon to the top of the pole, figure-eight the ends around the top two quads to secure.

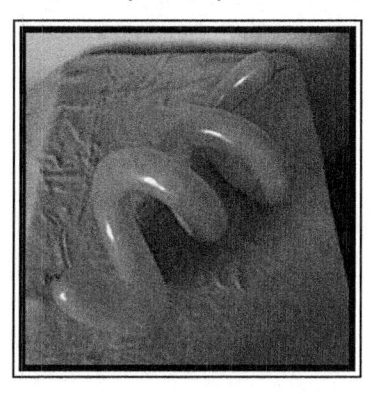

Now you are going to create a spiral to go around the exposed pole. Inflated a black 260 all the way and let the air out. Wrap the 260 around your hand, being careful not to twist. Inflate the 260 while holding it around your fingers. This creates a spiral.

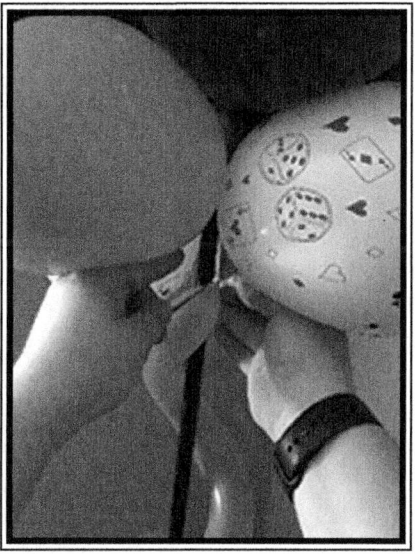

Tie the spiral to one of the nozzles in the 5" quad at the bottom of the centerpiece.

Follow the curve of the spiral to wrap the balloon around the pole. Tie it to one of the nozzles of the top 5" quad.

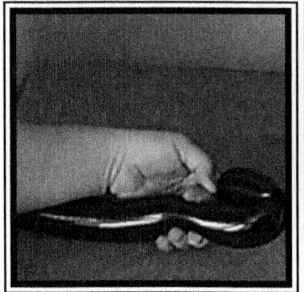

Take a partially inflated black 260. Twist a loop. Pull the nozzle through to secure. Make two more loops the same size. Do the same with the second and third partially inflated black 260.

Tie all three 260s together.

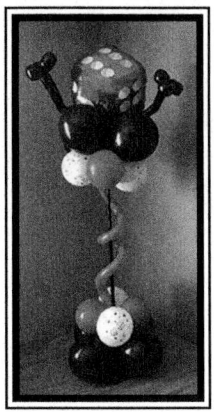

Bring the three 260s up underneath the black quads at the top of the centerpieces. Pull each one up between the red balloons so that they are standing up next to the die balloon.

Insert a card fan between the three loops in one of the 260s and secure with a sticky tab. Do the same on the other two 260s.

Stick more card fans onto the pole with sticky tabs. You can also stick them to the balloons. Do what looks good to you. Change the color scheme around for different looks. J

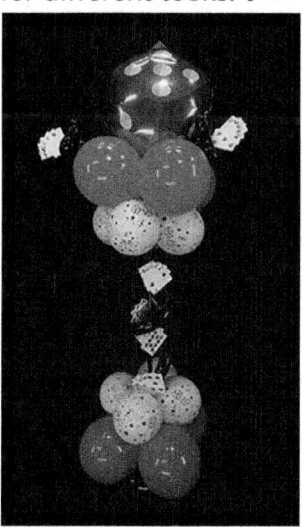

To See The Companion Video Go To:
https://youtu.be/-LT37oOI0WI

Casino Theme Balloon Arch

Materials:
- Balloon arch frame (made according to the balloon arch frame instructions), 4' EMT, 3 pieces of Uninflated 260 balloons
- 11" round balloons, black, in quads
- 11" round balloons, white, in quads
- 11" round balloons, red, in quads
- Casino themed Mylar balloons
- Sticky tabs

Start by creating garlands of quads to make it easier to pack your arch onsite.

142 www.DiyBalloonArt.com

Tie together two uninflated 260s. Tie this into a black quad. Figure-eight it around for security.

Wrap the uninflated 260s around your hand and hold taut. Place a second black quad on top of the first and figure-eight the uninflated 260 around it. Continue in this way until you have four quads of black.

Continue packing the garland in blocks of four quads of each color: black, white, red.

Make four garlands. You will have 12 quads on each garland.

To attach a garland onto your arch, place the garland near the arch frame and begin gently pulling the balloons around the frame one quad at a time. Twist two balloons from each quad around each other to secure.

Pay attention when switching from one garland to the next that you push the balloons close so that there are no gaps.

Once your arch is packed, use sticky tabs to attach Mylar balloons to the arch.

**To See The Companion Video Go To:
https://youtu.be/pquPRZtR_Ts**

Poker Chip Selfie Frame

Materials:
- Hula hoop, plastic
- 128* green 5" balloons sized to 4", quads
- 32* white 5" balloons sized to 4", quads
- Sticky tabs
- Numbers
- Card fans

*actual number of balloons depends on size of hoop, tension of packing and inflation size

Twist a green quad onto the hula hoop. Repeat with three more green quads.

www.DiyBalloonArt.com   145

Sandi Masori, CBA

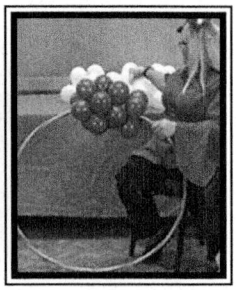

Twist on a white quad.

Continue adding quads to the hula hoop in the pattern, four green, one white until the hula hoop is full.

Use sticky tabs to attach a dollar sign and numbers to the frame for the chip value. The vinyl or cardboard cut out numbers work best.

Use sticky tabs to attach other embellishments, such as card fans.

146 www.DiyBalloonArt.com

The DIY Balloon Bible Themes & Dreams

To See The Companion Video Go To:
https://youtu.be/88hat4IY1Fc

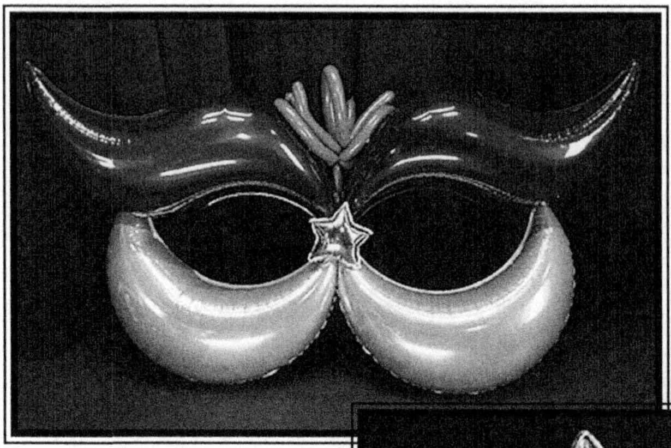

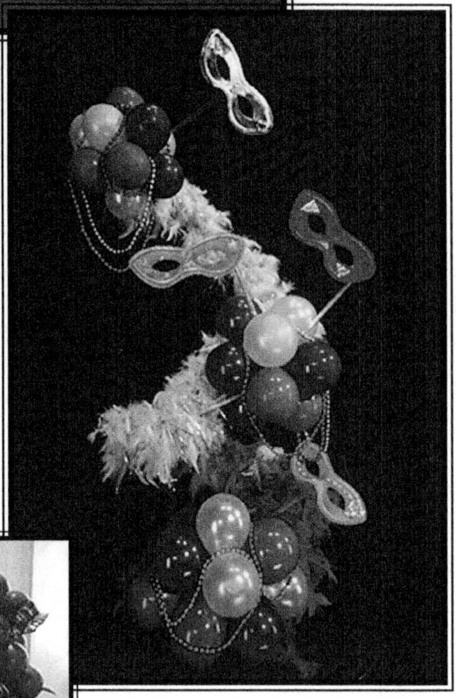

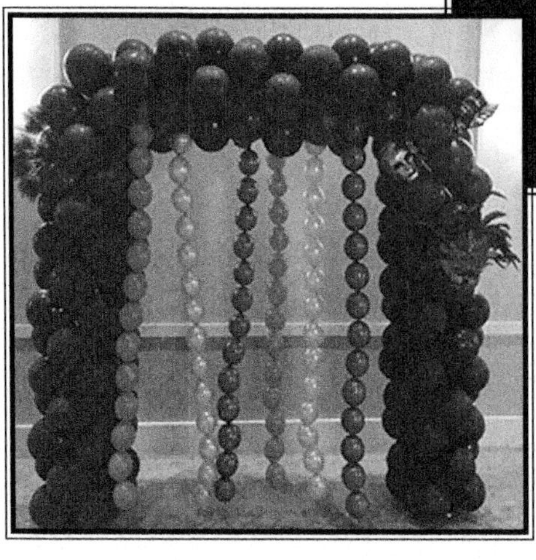

Mardi Gras Theme

Giant Mardi Gras Mask

Materials:
- 2 42" Curve balloon, purple
- 2 Jumbo Crescent balloon, gold
- 1 Small Star balloon, silver
- Two 260 balloons, green, fully inflated and burped
Sticky tabs

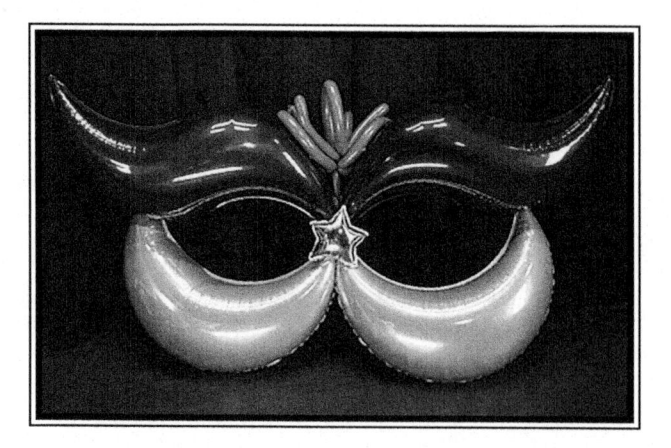

Warm your sticky tabs to body temperature before using.

Use sticky tabs to stick the two nozzles of the curves together.

Take the crescent balloons and decider where you want them for the mask. Attach the crescent with sticky tabs to the same place you've joined the curves. Do the second with the second crescent.

Use another sticky tab to secure the other ends of the crescents to the curve. Make sure you apply pressure until the tabs are secure.

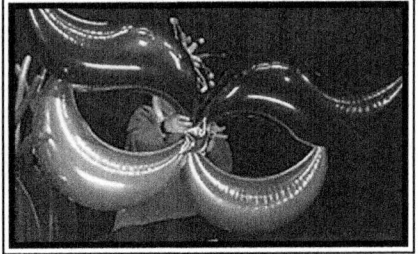

Attach the star with sticky tabs to the center point where you connected all four balloons to hide the connections.

Take a green 260. Fold it in half. Fold in half again and twist. This creates a ribbon shape. Repeat with a second 260.

Twist the two 260s together. These are your feathers.

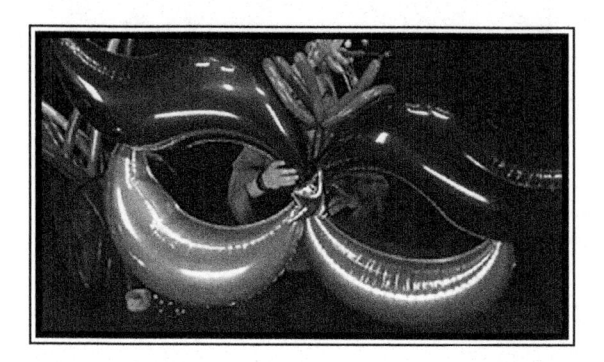

Use a sticky tab to secure one end of the 260s to the middle center of the mask. Secure with additional sticky tabs where needed.

To See The Companion Video Go To:
https://youtu.be/UYnWqaEtOUg

Mardi Gras Centerpiece

Materials:
- 10' Copper coil
- Twelve 5" balloons sized to 4", tied in duplets
- Twelve 5" balloons sized to 3", tied in duplets
- Twelve 5" balloons sized to 2", tied in duplets
- Two Feather boas
- Plastic bead necklaces
- Marti Gras masks
- straws

Adjust your copper coil so that it is balanced.

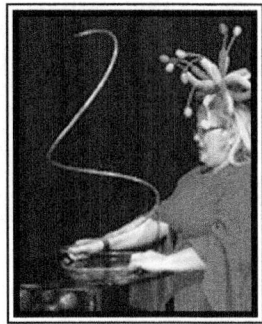

Twist together six 4" duplets to create a ball. Wrap the ball onto the copper coil near the bottom.

Twist together six 3" duplets to create a second ball. Wrap onto the cooper coil near the middle.

Create a third ball of duplets with the 2" balloons. Wrap onto the top of the copper coil.

The DIY Balloon Bible Themes & Dreams

Push the feather boa into the ball of balloons at the top. Wrap it around the wire, tucking into the bottom ball of balloons to secure. Do the same with a second boa.

Drape bead necklaces around balloons and pole.

Tape masks to straws. Stick straws into balloon balls wherever looks good to you.

www.DiyBalloonArt.com

155

Try not to put too much weight on the top of the centerpiece, as it may affect the balance.

To See The Companion Video Go To:
https://youtu.be/LYu9IaUSrA

Mardi Gras Beaded Arch

Materials:

- Frame:
  Two floor lamps 6'
  Two ½" elbow connectors
  5' ½" PVC
- 144 11" purple balloons sized to 8.5", quads
- Uninflated 260 balloons
- 6" Linky balloons in chains of 14
- Masks and feather to embellish to taste

First make garland to pack the frame. Tie together two uninflated 260s. Figure-eight the 260s into a purple quad. Place the quad on the floor, and wrap the 260 around your hand, so that you can hold it tight.

Place a second purple quad on top of the first, stretch the 260, figure-eight it around.

Repeat until you have filled your uninflated 260s with quads.

When you get to the end, figure-eight the 260 into the top two quads to secure. This is your garland for easier transport and creation of your arch. Make three garlands.

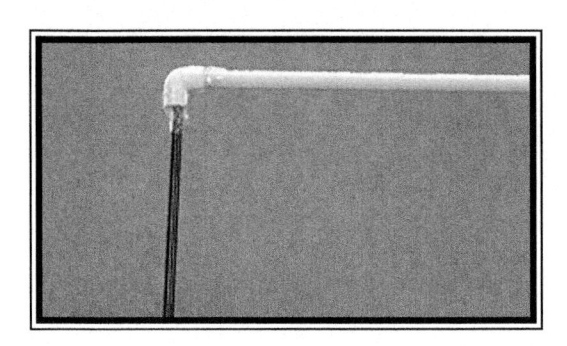

The frame is created by attaching an elbow connector to the top of two floor lamps, and inserting the PVC pipe into each elbow connector so that it is across the top.

Take one of the garlands of purple balloons and gently pull it onto one side of the frame, so that the pole is in the center.

Wrap a duplet around the pole at the corner to help fill out the corner and hide the pole.

Repeat on the other side of the frame.

Pull the third garland onto the top of the frame. This is your basic square arch.

To make the beads, tie together Linky balloons to create a chain. The number of balloons in your chain will depend on the height of your arch.

Make six chains.

Tie a piece of an uninflated 260 to the end of one of your chains, and the other end to a second chain.

Stretch the 260 over one of the balloons at the top of the arch, so that the chains hang down.

Repeat with all your chains to create a beaded curtain.

You can add in any embellishments to the arch that you want using 260s or sticky tabs.

To See The Companion Video Go To:
https://youtu.be/ikRYnZLPXIA

Sandi Masori, CBA

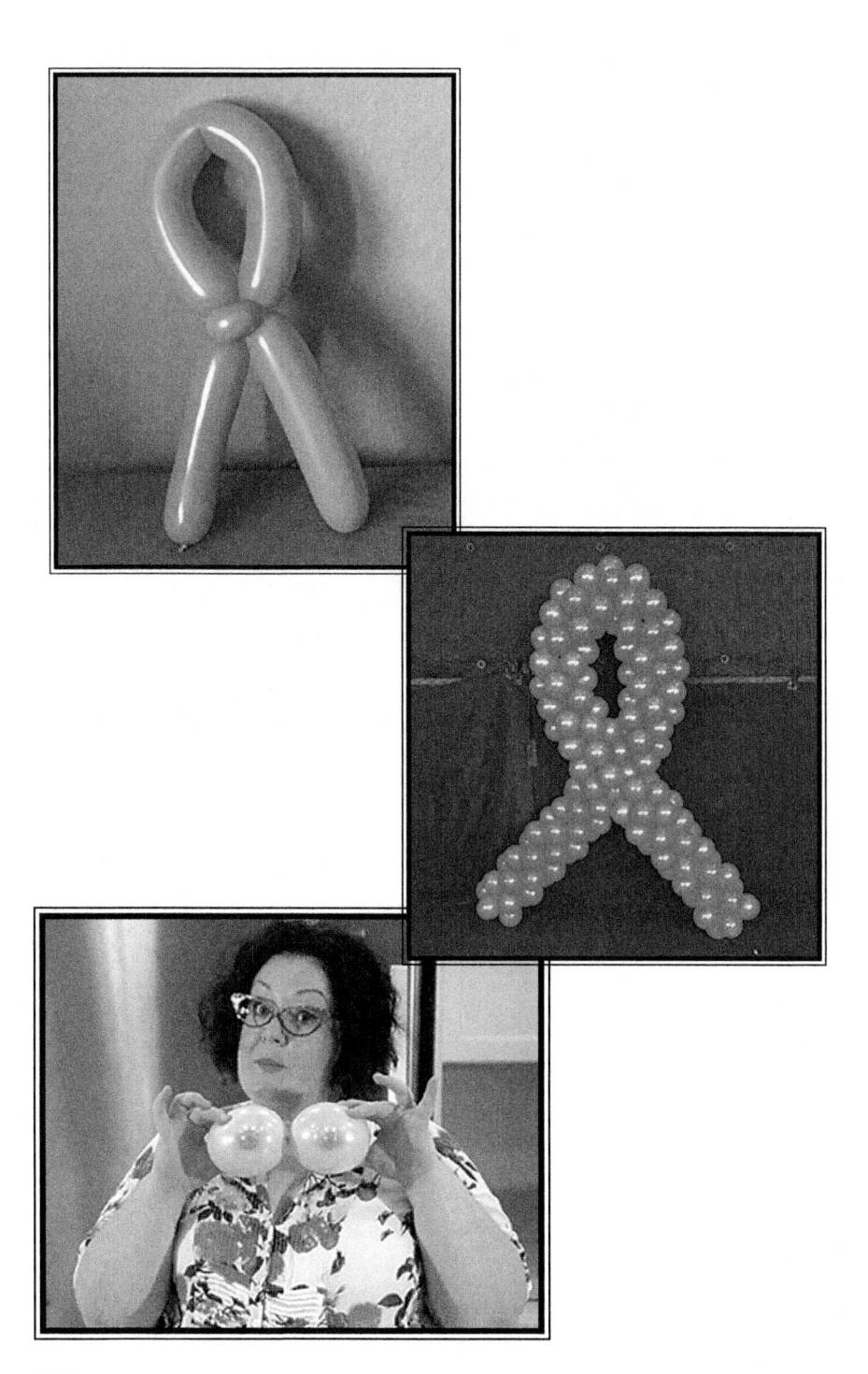

Awareness Themes

Mini Awareness Ribbon

Materials:

- One 260 balloon, inflated with small tail

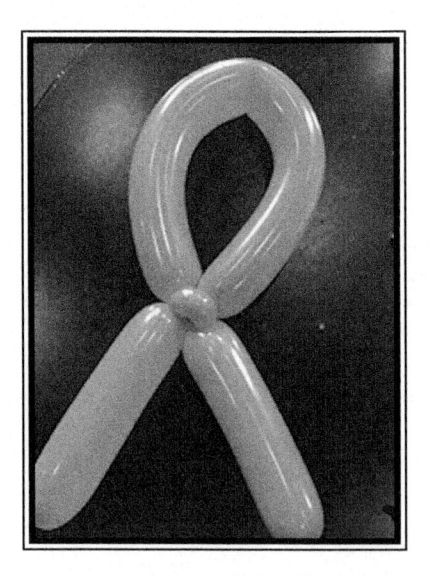

Fold the 260 to create a loop of the size you want. Squeeze and twist. Feed one end through the loop to secure.

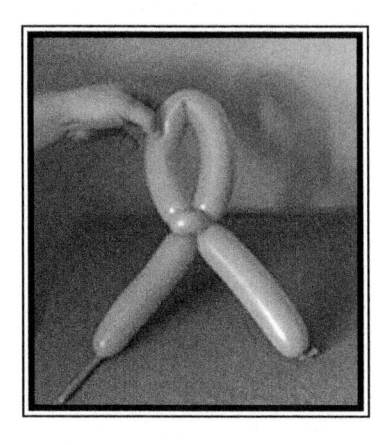

Make two pinch twists from the leg with the longest uninflated portion. Arrange so that one is in front of the loop and one in back. This will stabilize your ribbon.

Measure the longer ribbon end so that it matches the link of the other ribbon leg. Twist. Deflate while holding twist and tie off.

Trim ends.

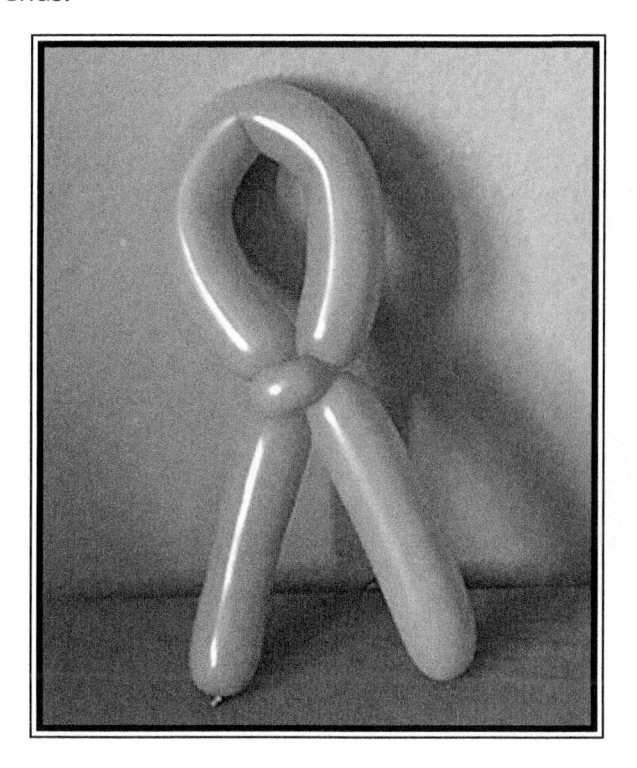

To See The Companion Video Go To:
https://youtu.be/jMNPj_w0lS8_

Giant Awareness Ribbon

Materials:
- 12' piece of aluminum rod, 3/16"
- 200 5" balloons sized to 4.5", in quads

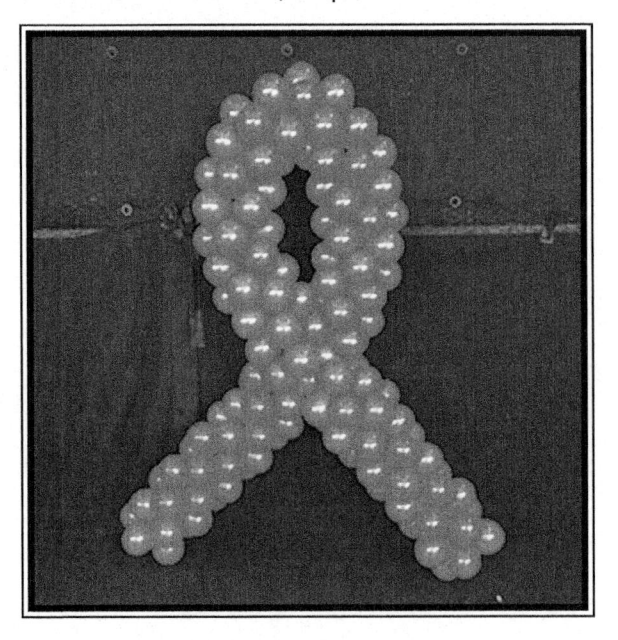

Tape off the ends of the aluminum rod.

Lay the rod flat.

Wrap a quad around one end of the pole.

Continue wrapping quads around the pole, nestling the balloons into each other, until you have filled the entire rod.

Hold the packed rod with the bend at the top. Cross the sides to make the ribbon shape.

Use an uninflated 260 to tie the two sides together to hold the shape.

If you want the shape more flush, cross the sides over, pop a few of the balloons, and nestle the front into the back.

To See The Companion Video Go To:
https://youtu.be/i3BfpjqdCtQ

Breast Cancer Awareness Breast Balloons

By Caity Byrne

Materials:
- 5" round, clear
- 5" round, blush
- 160 scrap, pink

Put your fingers into the clear 5" to open the nozzle. Push the pink 160 scrap inside. This is your nipple.

Push the blush balloon into the clear.

Inflate the clear balloon a few pumps.

Now make sure that both the blush and clear nozzles are over the pump and inflate the blush round.

When the blush is the size you want it, tie it off.

Move the pink scrap to the center.

Push the air out of the clear. It may help to cut off the nozzle of the blush. Squeeze as much air out as you can and work the pink scrap into the center where you want it.

To make a matching pair, tie two boobs together into a duplet.

This design looks awesome when tied into some balloons flowers as part of a "boobquet".

*Caity Byrne is the CEO of All About Balloons, a nationwide balloon décor and delivery service. To learn more about Caity or All About Balloons, go to http://www.AllAboutBalloons.com

To See The Companion Video Go To:
https://youtu.be/qiSyJx3vNVY

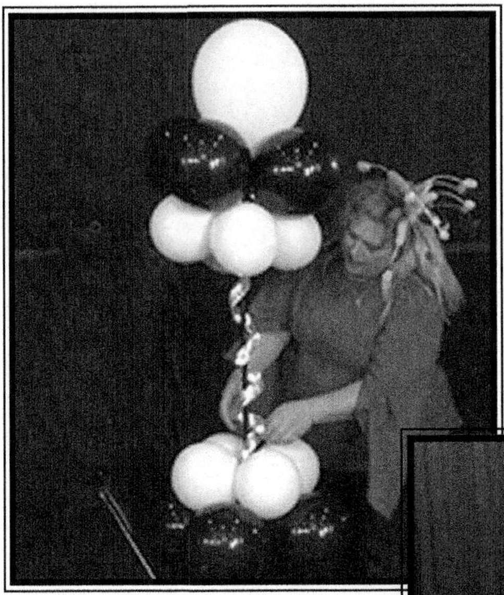

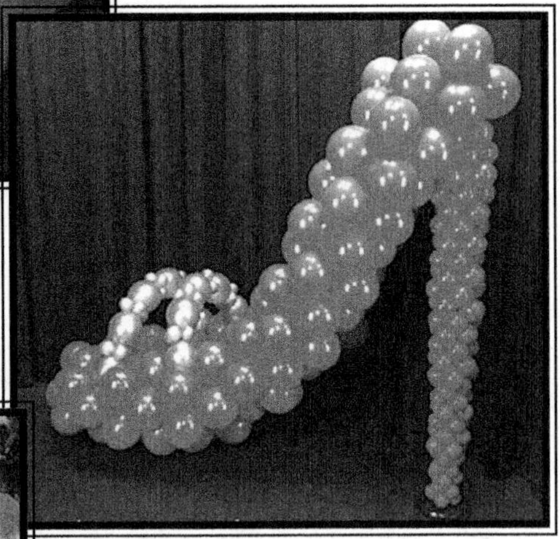

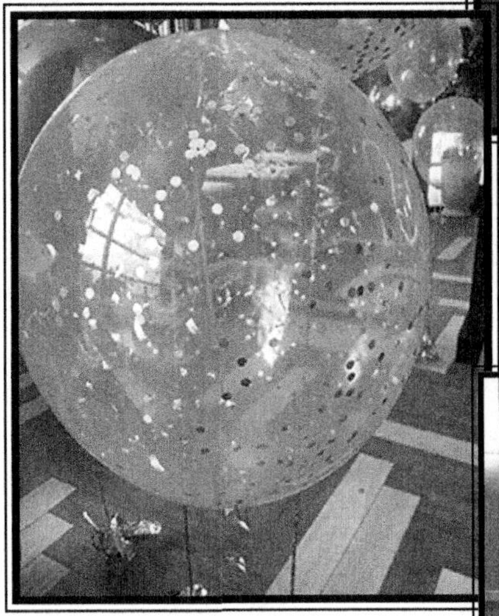

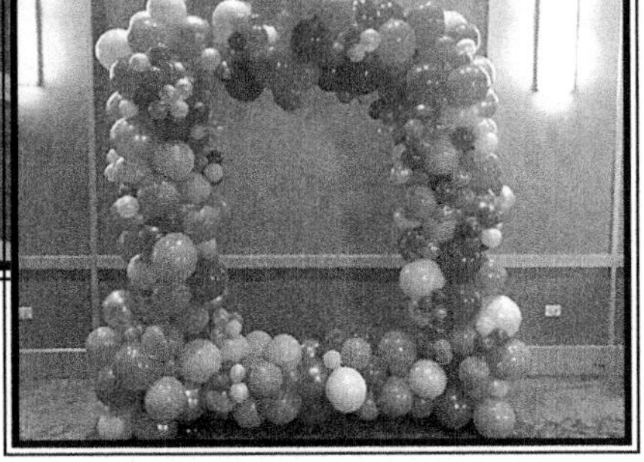

Elegant Themes / Events

Elegant Lighted Centerpiece

Materials:
- 8 11" balloons sized to 8", quads
- 8 11" balloons sized to 5", quads
- Lamp Base and pole
- Submersible color-changing balloon light
- Fishing line
- One white 16" balloon
  Ribbon lights

Wrap an 8" quad onto the base of the pole.

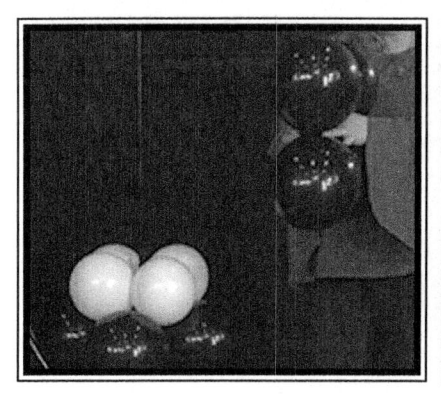

Wrap a 5" quad on top of the 8" quad.

Wrap an 8" quad onto the top of the pole.

Wrap a 5" quad directly below the 8" quad at the top.

On the base of the submersible balloon light there is a small hole. Feed fishing line through the hole and tie into a knot.

Stretch the neck of the 16" balloon and feed the balloon light in.

Inflate the 16" balloon, holding the fishing line to keep the light steady.

Stretch the neck white tightly pulling on the fishing line and tie the balloon. You want to make sure you are tying the fishing line into the neck of the balloon.

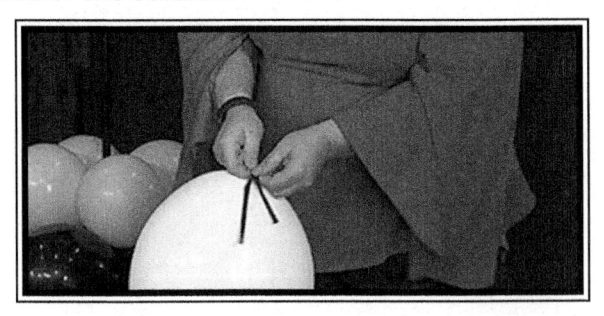

Tie an uninflated 260 to the neck of the 16" balloon, under the knot.

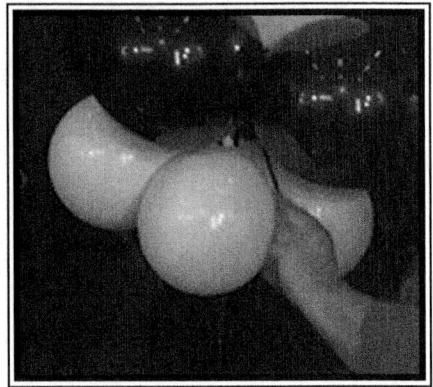

Tie the fishing line and the 260 together. This is a safety precaution so that if the balloon pops the light will not become a projectile.

Use the 260 to tie the 16" balloon to the top of the centerpiece pole. Wrap the 260 around and through the quads at the top to secure.

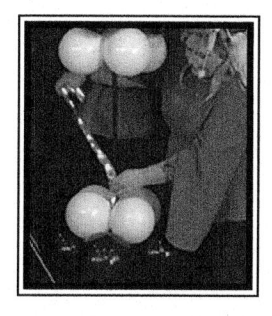

Tuck the battery pack for the lighted ribbon into the balloons at the base of the pole. Gently wrap the ribbon around the pole and tuck the end into the quads at the top.

*You can get the submersible color changing light and the ribbon lights from Fortune Products.

To See The Companion Video Go To:
https://youtu.be/jMcY-9oW7wl

High Heel Shoe

Materials:
- Uninflated 260 balloons
- 200 11" balloons inflated to 8", tied in duplets
- Lamp base
- 24 5" balloons sized to 2", tied in quads
- 40 5" balloons sized to 2" (in the same color as the linky balloons)
- 24 5" balloons sized to 3", tied in quads
- 24 5" balloons sized to 4", tied in quads
- 24 5" balloons sized to 4.5", tied in quads
- 24 5" balloons sized to 5", tied in quads
- 10 12" Linky balloons sized to 8"

Start by making a long long garland of balloons, about 25'. To make the garland, take two uninflated 260s tied together.

Twist together two 8" duplets to make a quad.

You are going to use the uninflated 260s as the center to wrap your quads, just like building a column.

Wrap the first quad onto the end of one of the uninflated 260s, wrapping the 260 around the center of the quad in a figure eight to secure.

Tighten the 260, place the next quad on top of the first, and wrap the 260 around it in a figure eight to secure. Repeat this process, tying in new 260s as you reach the end, until you have a garland of 25 quads.

The heel of the shoe is a simple column. Beginning packing the bottom of the base with the smallest set of quads, gradually increasing the size of the balloons as you move up the pole to create the stiletto shape.

Take the long garland you created and bring the ends next to each other, so that it is folded in half. Use the 260s inside to secure the sides together.

Tie the end you connected to the top of the heel using an uninflated 260. Figure eight the 260 into the top few quads of the heel to secure.

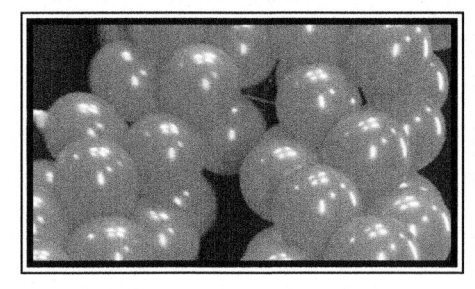

Using uninflated 260s tie the two sides of the garland together in a few places.

Use 8" quads to fill in the space in the center of your shoe. This will fill out the toe and give more of a shoe shape. This will be trial and error based on the size of your balloons and the size of your shoe.

Tie together Linky balloons to create a chain of six.

Wrap 2" quads between each set of Linky balloons to make the chain stiffer.

Figure eight the tail of one Linky balloon to the side of the shoe at the toe end. Bring the chain across the toe and secure at the opposite side as well. Tie the chain to the nozzle of one of the 9.5" balloons making up the base of the shoe. This is your toe strap.

To make a double toe strap, create a chain of five Linky balloons and secure to the shoe behind the first strap. Tie the chain to the nozzle of one of the 9.5" balloons making up the base of the shoe.

You could also use a chain of Linky balloons to create an ankle strap at the top of the shoe.

To See The Companion Video Go To:
https://youtu.be/5TX7iOO1Fg0

Glitter Balloon

Materials:

- Curling ribbon, cut into small pieces
- Or glitter, or confetti dots
- Hi float
- 16" clear balloon
- Helium tank

Use Hi Float on the clear balloon.

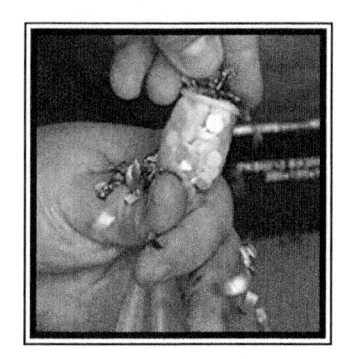

Hold the balloon at the base of the neck. Fill the neck with pieces of ribbon. Stuff as much as you can while holding the base so that the glitter doesn't fall down into the body of the balloon.

Carefully put the balloon onto the helium tank without losing too much ribbon. The force of the helium filling the balloon will spread the ribbon pieces all over the sides of the balloon. The Hi Float will act as a glue to keep the pieces on the walls of the balloon.

Shake the balloon to get a more even distribution of the ribbon pieces and get what was in the neck out.

Finish inflating the balloon. Tie off and attach curling ribbon to the nozzle.

To See The Companion Video Go To:
https://youtu.be/3up0BqyKvi8

Champagne Demi Arch

Materials:

- 300 11" balloons, random sizes, shades of blush, pink, clear
- 350 5" balloons, random sizes, shades of blush, pink, clear
- uninflated 260s
- Champagne bottle Mylar balloon
- 7" EMT, bent
- ¼" Aluminum rod
- Base plate (see section on how to make a column frame)

When inflating the balloons, make sure to keep them round, rather than egg shaped. They are meant to be champagne bubbles.

Tie balloons into duplets of random colors and sizes.

Grab two random duplets and twist into a quad. Tie to the end of an uninflated 260.

Create a second quad and place it above the first quad, wrapping the 260 around it to secure.

Continue to pack quads onto the uninflated 260s to create a garland.

Create garlands with all your 11" balloons.

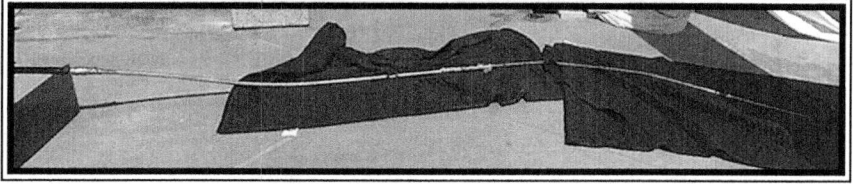

Secure the EMT to the base plate. Tape the aluminum rod to the EMT. This is the base for your demi arch.

Wrap a garland of 11" balloons onto the frame, starting at the bottom. Continue adding garlands until you reach the end of your frame. The garland piece will extend past the pole.

Don't worry about gaps, because you can fill them in later.

Tie another garland piece into the arch using the uninflated 260 in the center. Make sure to tie it to the aluminum rod as well.

Tie a final garland piece onto the end.

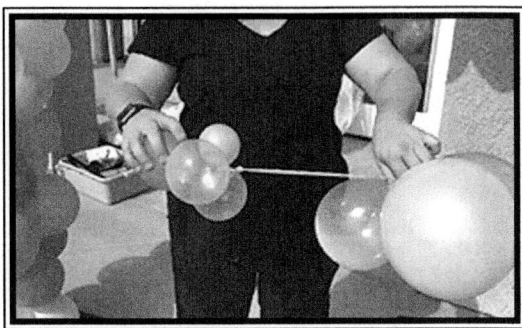

Make a quad of random size 5" balloons. Tie half of an uninflated 260 to the nozzles of one of the balloons in the quad. Tie the other end to a second quad.

Stretch the uninflated 260 and put it into the arch, so that the quads are on either side.

Repeat with the other 5" balloons, placing them to create the look of a spill of champagne.

Manicure the garland into the shape that you want, and attach to rig points on wall or ceiling for extra strength.

Tie the Champagne Mylar balloon to the last 11" quad, so that it is at the very top of the demi arch.

To See The Companion Video Go To:
https://youtu.be/OSFBlKqGx9o

Jumbo Color - Changing Balloon Lights

Materials:
- Remote Controlled Submersible Lights
- Fishing line
- 3' balloon
- Helium
  Weight

Once you have batteries in the light. Test it with the remote to make sure it is working correctly.

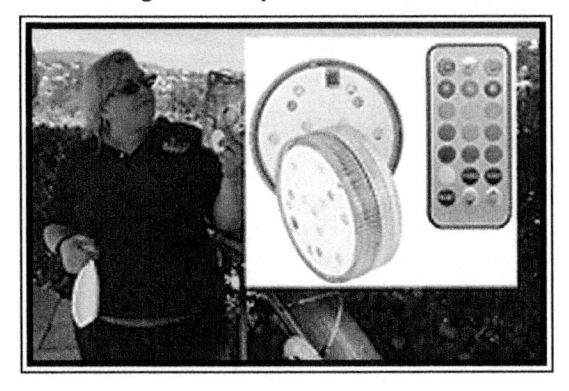

Tie fishing line through the small hole in the light.

Stretch the neck of the balloon open and push the light into the balloon.

Use the remote to turn the light on.

Hold the light at the base of the balloon light with one hand and the fishing line with the other. Place the neck of the balloon onto the helium tank.

Count the seconds that you hear the helium. Do the same amount in each balloon to make them all the same size.

Pull the fishing line and the neck of the balloon tight at the same time. Wrap around your hand and pull through to knot.

Before you pull your hand out of the knot, feed the shorter end of the fishing line through the knot partway.

Tie a knot that secures the fishing line from the light to the line that is anchoring the balloon.

Remove your hand. Grab all three fishing line strings and pull really tightly on the neck of the balloon.

Cut the neck off of the balloon. Trim the shorter ends of fishing line.

Measure the fishing line to the length that you want and tie it to your weight.

*Lights available from Fortune Products.

You can also fill them with air and use on top of pedestals or columns. ;-)

To See The Companion Video Go To:
https://youtu.be/hnrd926HNck

Organic Photo Frame – Full Size

Materials:
- 11" balloons, inflated to various sizes
- 5" balloons, inflated to various sizes
- Uninflated 260 balloons
- Photo frame base
  Two lamp poles
  Two 5" lengths of ½" or ¾" PVC
  Two T connectors
  Two elbow connectors

Create quads from random sizes of 11" balloons.

Tie together two uninflated 260s. Take an 11" quad and wrap the 260 around the center. Figure-eight it to secure.

Wrap the 260s around your hand and place the quad on the floor, holding the 260 taut. Place an 11" quad on top of the first and figure-eight the 260 around it to secure. Continue packing the 260 in this way to create a garland.

Make four garlands. This makes the balloons easier to transport and put together onsite.

Take one of the garlands you made and push it down onto the frame so that the pole runs through the center. If the garland is too long for the side, you can cut the 260 to remove the extra quads. Use pieces of uninflated 260s to tie the balloons to the pole to secure.

Do the same on the other three sides of the frame.

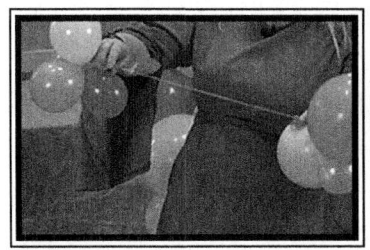

Twist together two duplets of 5" balloons into a quad. Cut an uninflated 260 in half. Tie to one of the nozzles of the quad. Create another quad of the odd sized 5" balloons. Tie the other end of the 260 half to the second quad. Stretch the 260 between the two quads and place it into the frame where desired.

Continue creating sets of quads and adding them to the frame until you have a look you like.

You can add silk flowers, lights, or greenery for embellishment.

To See The Companion Video Go To:
https://youtu.be/1WeDBJKVmP0

Appendix & Resources

To get the **bonus** material, videos and glossary, visit http://BalloonUtopia.com/ThemesDreams and fill out the form. This will trigger the automated system to send you a private link to the bonus material. I'm not even going to tell you what all the bonuses are, it's like a grab bag, you don't know what you're going to get until you open it up. And then it's awesome ;-)

The balloon lights can be purchased from Fortune Products, http://www.fortuneproducts.com

In the balloon business or want to be? Check out our Balloon Business Bootcamp. Http://www.BalloonCourse.com

Did I mention our awesome Facebook communities?? You should definitely join them! One is for DIY-ers and the other is for beginning balloon professionals. They are called: DIY Balloon Art and Beginning Balloon Professionals. If you do a Facebook search you should easily find them. We'd love to have you. ☺

Guest Contributors

Caity Byrne is the CEO of All About Balloons Inc. (Http://www.AllAboutBalloons.com), a national balloon décor and delivery company. She is an award winning balloon artist and instructor whose incredible installations have taken her into such exclusive places as The White House.

John Justice from Splendid Balloons (Http://www.SplendidBalloons.com) is an international award winning balloon artist from Colton, Ca and a Qualatex instructor.

Darren Saari from Twiisted Balloons (http://www.TwiistedBalloons.com) is an up and coming balloon artist who is being sought after to teach at balloon conventions and workshops.

About The Author

Sandi Masori, CBA wears many hats; professional balloon artist, marketer, educator, author, serial dieter, mother, and tv personality. Her passions are balloon art, travel, and online/ offline marketing.

Sandi grew up in San Diego, Ca and after traveling around the world making balloons, she returned to San Diego, where she now lives with her two children.

When Sandi is not writing books, or making videos, she runs Balloon Utopia (and Market With Balloons)- a San Diego based balloon decor and entertainment company, and The Masori Group, a San Diego based online/ offline marketing company. She also coaches and mentors marketing consultants and small business owners. Since the fall of 2013 Sandi has been invited to appear on numerous local and national TV shows, including The Today Show and multiple appearances on Hallmark's Home and Family Show. The media has been calling her "America's Top Balloon Expert." To see clips of her media appearances, visit her BalloonExpert website (http://www.BalloonExpert.com) .

Masori also run a popular YouTube channel (Sandiballoon), where she teaches DIYers, Crafters and Balloon Professionals how to make Balloon Decorations and Balloon Art.

In the precious spare time that she has between juggling those interests, Sandi likes to hang out with her family, read books, see movies, travel and hunt for the best Sushi in town.

Sandi can be reached at Sandi@BalloonUtopia.com. Her YouTube channel can be found at

Http://www.YouTube.com/Sandiballoon .

Printed in Great Britain
by Amazon